DOING
CONTEXTUAL
THERAPY

By the Same Author

Contextual Family Therapy:
Assessment and Intervention Procedures

A NORTON PROFESSIONAL BOOK

DOING CONTEXTUAL THERAPY

AN INTEGRATED MODEL FOR WORKING WITH INDIVIDUALS, COUPLES, AND FAMILIES

Peter Goldenthal, Ph.D. ABPP

W.W. Norton & Company, Inc.
New York · London

Library of Congress Cataloging-in-Publication Data

Goldenthal, Peter, 1948–
    Doing contextual therapy : an integrated model for working with
individuals, couples, and families / Peter Goldenthal.
        p.   cm.
    "A Norton professional book."
    Includes bibliographical references and index.
    ISBN 0-393-70208-1
    1. Contextual therapy.   2. Contextual therapy—Case studies.
I. Title.
RC488.55.G653   1996
616.89′14—dc20   95-42742 CIP

W. W. Norton & Company, Inc., 500 Fifth Avenue, New York, NY 10110
W. W. Norton & Company, Ltd., 10 Coptic Street, London WC1A 1PU

1 2 3 4 5 6 7 8 9 0

To the Memory of my Grandparents
Lillian Hochberg Bleich and Abraham H. Bleich
Betty Segal Goldenthal and Moses Goldenthal

CONTENTS

ACKNOWLEDGMENTS

Many people have contributed to this book, some without knowing that they had done so. The integrative nature of the contextual model has given me an opportunity to draw on clinical and conceptual knowledge shared with me by many teachers, mentors, and supervisors, especially Ronald Mack at Cornell; George Allen, Amerigo Farina, Irving Kirsch, Donald Mosher, and Julian B. Rotter at the University of Connecticut; and Pauline B. Hahn at Judge Baker Guidance Center.

This book grew directly out of my study and discussions with Ivan Boszormenyi-Nagy, founder of the contextual approach. But my debt to him exceeds that of student to teacher; I have benefitted as much personally as professionally from his generously shared wisdom and kind support over the past decade. I have also benefitted from many discussions with numerous contextual therapy colleagues, especially Jeff Cebula, Catherine Ducommun-Nagy, Larry Fader, Vincent Gioe, Judith Grunebaum, Ellie Horgan, and John Quintana. Judith Grunebaum also read the entire manuscript in draft form and offered many valuable suggestions. Wendy Merron Goldenthal developed the concept for the book's cover art. More general discussions with colleagues Steve Berk, Richard Cruz, Linda Knauss, John Mc-Brearty, Len Milling, Paul Rappoport, and Virginia Wilking have enriched this book considerably. Interacting with, and responding to questions posed by students, supervisees, and seminar and workshop participants over the years has been very helpful in anticipating possible points of confusion and in refining explanations and illustrations of contextual concepts and techniques.

It is one thing to have a vision of a book and quite another to realize that vision. Susan Barrows Munro and Regina Dahlgren Ardini, editors at Norton Professional Books, have been my trustworthy and reliable guides throughout this exhilarating adventure. Their combined expertise has been of immense help in keeping my original vision in focus and in finding a voice to share it with my readers.

Even with the contributions of wise colleagues and expert editors, the book would quite literally not have been possible were it not for the patience, tolerance, encouragement, and support of my wife, Wendy, and children, Ariel, Matthew, Rebecca, and Sara: Thank you all.

INTRODUCTION

Contextual therapy has become a model of human experience, family life, and therapy whose goals are widely admired, whose assumptions are widely endorsed, and whose concepts are widely borrowed. It is difficult to find an experienced therapist who would argue with the notion that knowledge of a person's past and present family relationships is crucial to understanding and helping the person, or one who would deny that issues of loyalty and fairness are central to life and to close relationships.

But many who would practice contextual therapy, and many more who would incorporate contextual concepts such as *loyalty* or *destructive entitlement* or treatment strategies such as *multidirected partiality* into their work feel that this practice is shrouded in mystery. At workshops and seminars therapists of all stripes talk about contextual therapy as a "wonderfully philosophical" approach or comment to each other about its complexity or the difficulty of turning its "theoretical concepts" into action. Private practitioners worry about how to use a "family therapy" method with the individuals who occupy at least half of their office time. Those with a practical bent also wonder how they would explain the approach to managed care gate-keepers. Those in the public or private nonprofit sector express concern about how to use an approach they believe to be committed to very long-term therapy, or one which they believe is only suited to psychologically sophisticated clients. Others whose practices center on helping families with young children or adolescents wonder how one can possibly talk to children about such abstract and seemingly philosophical ideas as fairness.

I am neither philosopher nor theorist, but a clinician trying to help those individuals, couples, and families who call me hoping for support, some alleviation of their suffering, and some resolution of their interpersonal difficulties. After working for many years to find a way to integrate the most useful aspects of what I had learned about the psychology of individuals with what was positive about the currently popular family therapies, I discovered that a solution to my dilemma already existed. In the twelve years that I have been studying and using the contextual approach it has been consistently useful, often well beyond my expectations.

My clinical experience has covered the spectrum from working in the public sector with multiproblem families with young children and with very severe symptoms in several family members, to working in private practice with other therapists seeking personal and professional growth, and including nearly every possible sort of situation in between. Neither the conceptual model, the basic principles, nor the clinical techniques have varied in working with this highly diverse group of individuals and families. The basic principles have always been to try as much as possible to consider the impact of the therapy on all the people who might be affected by it, to help people look for opportunities to give to each other and to acknowledge each others' efforts to give, and so to focus on resources for building trust rather than on pathology.

In this book, as in my workshops and in supervision, I have emphasized the clinical and practical doing of contextual therapy, touching only briefly on the theoretical underpinnings of the model. As is well known, the contextual therapy model owes its birth to the work of Ivan Boszormenyi-Nagy and his colleagues and it is in their writings that the interested reader will find the deepest and most detailed expositions of its conceptual framework and intellectual foundations (e.g., Boszormenyi-Nagy, 1965, 1987; Boszormenyi-Nagy, Grunebaum, & Ulrich, 1991; Boszormenyi-Nagy & Krasner, 1986; Boszormenyi-Nagy & Spark, 1973). Those looking for a brief theoretical overview of the approach may also find the work of Goldenthal (1993) and van Heusden and van den Eerenbeemt (1987) of interest.

This book aims to answer practitioners' clinical and practical questions, all of which are variations on a theme: What is contextual therapy really about? What does it set out to accomplish? What do contextual therapists try to change or to help people change for themselves? What do contextual therapists actually do, and how can I use these techniques to help my patients*? The aim here is not to discuss each and every concept that has been developed by those working from this perspective. Rather, the goal is to illustrate those concepts and methods that I have found most useful and those that can most readily be combined with a variety of other therapeutic approaches. Rather than scan a large number of concepts briefly, I shall focus in detail on a select few. Each of the concepts or methods will be defined and illustrated with several clinical vignettes.

---

*None of the many possible ways to refer to those who seek our professional services fits all people at all times. I realize that among some clinicians the term "patient" conjures up images of a dominant, perhaps even arrogant, doctor and a subservient, passive patient. According to *Ayto's Dictionary of Word Origins* (1990), however, the word "patient" is derived from a Latin and old French root meaning "one who suffers." To my mind this is a better fit with reality than is the alternative "client," a word derived from the Latin *cliens*, someone of low rank whose task it is to listen, follow, and obey. Neither is the more modern meaning of client as a "customer" sufficiently specific for our purposes here.

THE ANSWER TO THREE
PROBLEMS IN CLINICAL WORK

I came to this way of thinking about clinical work as the result of being confronted by a number of problems that I believe are shared by many clinicians. One of these problems is how to conceptualize our work in a way that encompasses what we know about individual psychological functioning with what we know about family systems. Until fairly recently these represented two warring camps who rarely spoke to each other. Fortunately, this is much less true today, but the problem of how to integrate them remains alive.

Another problem that faces many clinicians is how to establish working relationships with all family members. Whether we call it a therapeutic alliance or rapport or something else, it is a crucial aspect of our work and can be a damnably difficult thing to do when working with a couple or family in which there is disagreement, tension, conflict—in other words, the kind of couples and families who seek therapy. In the following pages I will discuss one way of handling this very difficult task, and even go a step beyond by taking into account other people we never actually see in the therapy room but who are probably going to be affected by what goes on there.

Finally, all therapists are faced with the problem of finding a way to make sense of the unfortunate reality that people who genuinely care about and love their families—their spouses, their parents, and their children—still at times find themselves in situations where they have done something that has caused hurt to just those people they care about the most. And we therapists are left trying to find some way of understanding how this can be, how people can care about each other and yet hurt each other. And more than that, we are left with the hard job of finding a way to make sense of this that will help us to promote growth and caring in families, that will be helpful to families. We need to be diagnose any significant psychological difficulty that is present—of course, this is part of treatment—but we need to go beyond this to find an explanation of how it can arise. And these questions confront us whether we typically work with families with young children, with couples, or with adults who are trying to improve their relationships with their own parents. The contextual approach offers one way of making sense of this very difficult facet of life. It also helps therapists meet the extremely difficult challenge of establishing working alliances with the very people whose actions have caused injuries to others, simultaneously helping those who have been injured to give voice to their grievances and to risk reengaging with those who have wronged them.

The book is designed to be a workshop between covers. Methods and techniques will be described and illustrated in detail. Procedures that vary depending on whether the therapist is in a room with an individual, with a couple, or with a family with young children or adolescents will be addressed explicitly. Some procedures are used without changes with different patient groupings; these will be noted as well. The book is in two major sections: The first discusses contextual therapy concepts and techniques, illustrating them with brief clinical vignettes; the second presents a study of brief contextual therapy, including family sessions with a ten-year-old boy and his parents, individual sessions with his mother, and a three-year follow-up. If I have succeeded in my goal in writing this book, each reader should feel that he or she is able to apply at least some of the techniques and procedures described here with his or her next patient.

Author's Note

This book contains many clinical illustrations, each of which has been disguised to protect the privacy of the people involved. Many of the cases and session excerpts featured in Part One are composites, combining clinical features from a number of similar cases; other vignettes are drawn from actual sessions in which identifying details have been highly disguised. Part Two features a detailed case presentation; the procedure for safeguarding the privacy of this family is discussed in the introduction to that section.

DOING
CONTEXTUAL
THERAPY

PART ONE

≈

CONCEPTS AND TECHNIQUES

1

THE CONTEXTUAL APPROACH

Let's consider one of the questions mentioned in the introduction: What does the contextual approach try to change? The broad goals are to help people who seek therapy, whether as part of a family group, a dyad, or as individuals, make fundamental changes in the ways they think about their relationships, and in the ways they act in those relationships, with the aim of moving toward greater balance. One fundamental goal is to help people begin to change in ways that facilitate their abilities to acknowledge each other's positive efforts. Whenever the therapist acknowledges either the positive efforts or past injuries of one person, the purpose of doing so is to facilitate people's abilities to acknowledge each other's efforts and contributions to the relationship; the therapist's acknowledgment is not an end product, but a catalyst for further change. Beginning with the first session the therapist looks for ways to give credit to people in order to help them give credit to each other. As people begin to do this, both the one acknowledged and the one who does the acknowledging benefit significantly. This approach recognizes that pathology exists in both individuals and families, but its emphasis is on optimizing resources and catalyzing future growth.

HIGHLIGHTING FAIRNESS ISSUES

This approach seeks to highlight fairness as a major issue in all close relationships and to help people to talk with each other in ways that both help them to state their own sides in a conflict and to be able to truly hear the other person's side. The therapist helps people to think and talk about what is fair and unfair by highlighting the issue in the very first session. It is extraordinarily difficult to define a concept like "fairness." It is nonetheless a crucial concept, not only in this approach, but also in all relationships. I cannot adequately define what fairness means or even stipulate what constitutes a fair relationship or what fair compromises among people in close relationships are. There are, however, some things that I believe can readily be agreed upon; for example, infants and young children deserve love, nurturance, protection, as well as trustworthy parents who do not use them to meet their unmet emotional or physical needs in harmful ways; any violation of this would clearly represent unfairness. Children also deserve to be free to love and show their love for both of their parents, regardless of whether those parents are happily married, unhappily divorced, or have never been married. It is clearly unfair for children of any age to be constrained so that loving one parent represents disloyalty to the other. Similarly, adults can rightfully expect that their relationships will balance out over time—that they will receive back in fair measure what they have given.

Fairness issues and their implications are inherent in this approach and dictate therapists' activities from beginning assessments through termination sessions. They provide the foundation for the relationship between therapists and patients. They govern the questions we ask our clients and patients. They guide our thinking about what may have caused problems and what may be done to ameliorate them. They provide a context for understanding and integrating patterns of family communication and power transactions, historical information (both personal and intergenerational), and psychological issues. Observing, thinking about, and helping people think and talk about fairness provides the overall principle that creates the possibility for an integrative framework. The overarching concern with fairness leads to a model that can incorporate concepts, procedures, or techniques from any other therapeutic model as long as they are consistent with this concern for helping people to enhance the quality of their most important relationships.

THE IMPORTANCE OF HISTORY

Helping people to move forward often depends on understanding not just their present difficulties, but also their past experiences, particularly those that caused them pain and injury. We seek information about people's prior experiences, not because we wish to become archaeologists of the mind, but because we want to understand them, especially the ways they have been hurt, so that we may help them develop new ways of experiencing and relating. In order to be partial to all family members we need to know about the things that have hurt each of them earlier in their lives. In the language of contextual therapy, we need to know about their personal histories of experienced unfairness and injustice. Some aspects of people's histories are strictly individual, some refer to their families, and some apply to members of their race, gender, or cultural group. The emphasis on understanding history shares much with other approaches that think about family issues over an intergenerational time frame (Levant, 1984). These "historical" approaches include the psychodynamic family therapies of Ackerman (1966), Framo (1976, 1982), and Wynne (1965), as well as the multigenerational approach of Bowen and his colleagues (Bowen, 1966; Kerr & Bowen, 1988).

INTEGRATING INDIVIDUAL
AND FAMILY SYSTEMS ISSUES

A third defining feature, and one that differentiates this approach from many others, is that it provides a framework for integrating concepts and techniques from diverse models of individual and family development, functioning, and therapy. Contextual therapy is based on the assumption that many personal and interpersonal problems will benefit from interventions that increase peoples' capacities for achieving greater balance in their most important relationships. It enthusiastically endorses the use of any and all techniques likely to benefit people as long as they are consistent with this goal; it seeks to be inclusive rather than exclusive (Boszormenyi-Nagy et al., 1991). For this reason, and despite its many historical ties to the family therapy movement and its leaders, the label of "family therapy" does not adequately reflect the actual scope of this approach. Contextual therapy is more accurately thought of as an integrative therapy (e.g., Garfield, 1994; Goldfried, 1980, 1982; Norcross & Goldfried, 1992). While there is considerable variation in the way the terms are used (Garfield, 1994), Stricker's (1994) description of *theoretical integration*, as "an attempt to understand the patient by developing a superordinate theoretical framework that draws from a variety of different frameworks (p. 5)" appears to fit the four-dimensional contextual model relatively well with one exception: In contextual therapy the superordinate framework is not theoretical, but ethical. The fundamental defining goal is to help people be more considerate in their relationships with those closest to them, give more spontaneously and freely of themselves to those in their families, and state their own needs and wishes in a spirit of open dialogue.

Family systems concepts as discussed by Boszormenyi-Nagy's colleagues among the first generation of family therapy theoreticians, practitioners, and researchers, including Jackson (1957), Bowen (1978), Wynne (e.g., Wynne, Ryckoff, Day, & Hirsch, 1958), and Bateson and his colleagues (Bateson, 1972; Bateson,

Jackson, Haley, & Weakland, 1956), as well as more recent contributors such as Minuchin (1974), Haley (1976), and others, are fully compatible with this model. These systems concepts include patterns of communication among family members, triangulation, coalitions, boundaries within the family, boundaries between the family and the environment, family roles, and the potential for scapegoating, as well as issues of interpersonal power and control. Therapists' observations of these phenomena during sessions, as well as family members' reports of how they communicate and interact with each other receive careful attention in the contextual approach.

While this integrative approach and the so-called "classical family therapies," or family systems therapies, overlap to a certain extent, there are also significant differences between them. Thinking of families as systems can be very useful; it is important to remember, however, that these systems are made up of people who have thoughts, feelings, and complex inner lives. Individuals are systems too, not just cogs in a systemic wheel. A number of the earlier systems therapies actively rejected any notion of individual psychology, particularly of individual psychopathology, espousing instead a particularly unyielding form of systems thinking. The limitations of this approach are by now well-known and documented (e.g., Burbatti, Castoldi, & Maggi, 1993).

Failing to see each individual's personal concerns, feelings, thoughts, wishes, hopes, past hurts, and disappointments can lead one to make major errors when conducting couples and family therapy sessions as much as they can when working with an individual. People differ from each other in important ways. Some of these differences, such as ego strengths and weaknesses, character structure, ego defenses, and coping style, are emphasized by the psychodynamic tradition. Object relations and interpersonal issues, particularly those associated with Fairbairn, Sullivan, and others referred to by Greenberg and Mitchell (1983) as exemplifying the *relational/structural model*, are of great interest. Although generally associated only with the tradition of psychoanalytically oriented individual psychotherapy, issues related to both transference and countertransference are additional important psychological factors to consider in contextual therapy. Other important individual differences reflect difficulties in life that are experienced by people as individuals. Even in an approach that tries hard to focus on resources rather than on pathology, it must be recognized that some people with whom we work have very significant individual emotional and psychological difficulties; when a patient or family member is schizophrenic or suffers from a major depression or bipolar disorder, it needs to be recognized, acknowledged, and addressed.

The list of such potential contributors to a contextual therapist's palette of concepts related to individual psychological functioning is limited only to those that take people's welfare into account in a responsible manner—not by any theoretical bias or proscription built into the model. Contextual therapists energetically include any procedure or technique that may be helpful to people. In addition to psychoanalytically derived concepts such as those already mentioned, I frequently incorporate concepts drawn from Adler's individual psychology (1923, 1924, 1927), Rotter's social learning theory (1954), and Beck's cognitive behavior therapy (Beck, Rush, Shaw, & Emery, 1979). Each clinician will, of course, develop his or her own way of combining useful concepts and techniques for assessing individual psychological concerns, strengths, and weaknesses, as well as for addressing these issues using psychologically based interventions.

When children are included, the need to pay attention to individual psychological issues takes on added significance. It becomes important to assess and attend to developmental issues such as those discussed by Erikson (1963, 1968), Freud (1946), and Piaget (Flavell, 1977; Piaget, 1963; Piaget & Inhelder, 1969). Many of the children who are brought into therapy by their parents are having difficulties of one kind or another in school. In addition, parents may sometimes have specific questions about learning disabilities or hyperactivity. As therapists we may feel that such school problems are likely to reflect family issues, or perhaps parent-child issues. From the perspective offered here, however, it still makes a great deal of sense to pay attention to each child's cognitive strengths and weaknesses. We will also be alert to developmental difficulties such as those discussed by developmental pediatricians (e.g., Levine, 1991) and neuropsychologists (e.g., Hynd & Willis, 1988). In some cases informal evaluation, perhaps limited to asking some questions and observing the child or talking to teachers on the telephone, may be sufficient. In other cases formal psychological or neuropsychological evaluations as well as continuing collaboration with other professionals such as educators and pediatricians may be needed.

FOUR DIMENSIONS

The concerns with fairness, the psychological functioning of individuals, patterns of family communication, structure, and power, and learning about history are interrelated. Generally, all these aspects of people's lives are discussed more formally in terms of the following four dimensions: *dimension I* (objectifiable facts) treats issues of individual and family history; *dimension II* (individual psychology) includes what I have been referring to as individual issues; *dimension III* (systems of transactional patterns) encompasses family systems variables; and *dimension IV* (the ethic of due consideration or merited trust) treats fairness issues.

These terms may appear to describe four different and independent sets of concerns and issues. This is not the case. They are, rather, attempts to capture four highly overlapping, interconnected, and interwoven aspects of people's lives. In clinical practice many of the questions we ask about history, and much of what we observe about family transactions, have clear implications for understanding the capacities of family members to see each others' needs and hurts. Our concern with issues of fairness provides the glue that holds this integrative framework together. Like individual psychodynamically oriented therapists, we are interested in people's inner psychological functioning; however, we differ from them in our emphasis on interpersonal realities and our search for interconnections between fairness issues and psychological issues. Similarly, like family systems therapists, we observe and learn about patterns of family interactions, communication, structure, and power issues. We differ from the strictly systemic therapies in that our major interest is in relating what we learn about these features of family life to fairness issues.

MULTIDIRECTED PARTIALITY

Therapists who utilize contextual therapy are committed to trying to consider the welfare of all those people whose lives are likely to be affected by what happens during, and as the result of, therapy — even those they may never meet, for example, estranged or separated spouses, parents who no longer live with their children, and adults' cut-off siblings, parents, or grandparents. This concern for others who are likely to be affected by whatever changes are made as the result of therapy applies just as strongly when the patient is an individual. Individual patients often have spouses or adult partners, they sometimes have children and siblings, and they always have parents. All of these people and more will be affected by what happens between the therapist and the individual patient. Indeed, even children and grandchildren who are not yet born will be affected profoundly by these changes.

Contextual therapists are committed to being partial to each of these people and are prepared to take each of their sides when this is called for. But being partial to one person does not eliminate the need to be partial to others; one must be aware of each of these people and be prepared to be partial to each at different moments in therapy. What is required is not what might be called a unilateral partiality, the sort of thing advocated many years ago in traditional child guidance clinics whereby one worker took the child's side, another the side of the parent. Neither will impartiality, for example in the form of therapeutic neutrality as espoused by Selvini-Palazzoli and her colleagues (Selvini-Palazzoli, Boscolo, Cecchin, & Prata, 1978, 1980), do for our purposes.

What is needed instead is a multilateral partiality, a *multidirected partiality* that guides us to carefully consider each person's previous experiences, especially those that involve being exploited or otherwise subjected to unfair injury, as well as his or her current needs and feelings; and to lend our therapeutic weight to the person whose past injuries or current efforts to give to others call for our support the most at that moment. This does not mean that we always or frequently side with one person against another or against all others (although we may do this at times); rather, it means that we are prepared to do this in order to help people to speak their minds, to give to each other, to acknowledge each other's efforts, and to achieve more balanced relationships. We need not and should not strive to be equally partial to everybody at the same time; we need not strive to care equally about everyone at a specific moment. Rather, we strive to be open to the possibility of lending our therapeutic weight to each of the people who will be affected by the therapeutic process, those who are in the therapy room, and those who are not.

The meaning of this concept is perhaps best approached by breaking it down into its components: multi — directed — partiality, each having a common sense, everyday meaning. In general usage *multi* refers to many; *directed* here means "aimed toward"; and being *partial* means favoring someone or something as in, "I like all ice cream but I am partial to Ben and Jerry's Cherry Garcia." So multidirected partiality involves aiming (i.e., directing) one's favoritism (partiality) in multiple directions, or in the case of therapy, toward multiple people, not all at once but selectively.

In working with the S family (chapters 7–9), for example, I often choose to be partial to Dennis, an intellectually limited young child who has great difficulty expressing himself. At times I speak for him; at other times I direct his parents' attention to his strengths or to his positive efforts. In each instance I am motivated by a wish to increase each person's capacity to give to the others in his or her family. I may be partial to Dennis out of concern that he will stop trying to achieve and to contribute to his family if someone does not acknowledge his giving; I may do so to model how one may acknowledge a child's efforts, even if those efforts are not always successful.

Other cases throughout this book contain similar examples of following the principle of multidirected partiality by being partial to one person at a time. We do not do this in a predetermined manner; neither do we intentionally side with one person or another in order to unbalance a family system. Decisions about whose side to take are always based on clinical judgment about who has been harmed the most in the past in ways that interfere with their abilities to speak up for themselves or to respond with consideration to what another has to say. And each decision is made with full awareness that in the next session, or perhaps in the next moment, we will be encouraging another family member to talk about his or her needs, aspirations, hopes, or injuries, pushing another family member to consider a partner's or child's concerns more carefully. Multidirected partiality guides us to consider each person's perspective, and then to decide who needs our partiality at that moment. This is the most important guiding principle for the rest of this book and for the contextual approach to therapy with individuals, with couples, and with families.

A few comments about the term *multidirected partiality* may be useful. While writing this chapter I tried to make the concept easier to understand and more familiar by substituting shorter, nontechnical words; for example: "taking everybody's side," "being partial to everybody," "taking the side of the relationship," and many others. Each of these phrases conveys a piece of what multidirected partiality is about, but none of these substitutions adequately conveys the complexity of the concept. Each of these phrases is also potentially misleading, perhaps in ways that illuminate the difficulties inherent in discussing this core concept. Multidirected partiality does not guide us to be equally partial to *everybody*; we do not take sides as in an adversarial or litigious confrontation; neither do we side with a relationship as an abstract entity that exists apart from the people who are relating. It now seems to me that the strangeness of the term is not without benefit; it serves as a reminder that this concept is radically different from other views on the nature of the therapist's efforts on behalf of patients. The differences are both subtle and crucially important. No clinician can hope to fully utilize the leverage of the contextual approach without appreciating what it means to be partial in a multidirected way. Once adjusting to operating in this way, however, clinicians will master related contextual concepts smoothly and relatively quickly; doing contextual therapy will seem so natural that one will wonder what was so difficult at first.

Techniques of Multidirected Partiality

How can a therapist actually be partial to each person who will be affected by what happens in therapy? Many clinicians are already very familiar with the techniques that move it from being just an interesting idea to a powerful therapeutic tool. The basic techniques have been described most recently by Boszormenyi-Nagy et al. (1991). The first and most familiar technique is that of empathy. All therapists experience and express their empathy in response to patients' or clients' pain, loss, anxieties, and life difficulties. This approach is no different in this regard. To stifle one's natural human response to another's past or present suffering is unlikely to be therapeutic in any sense. To share these feelings, to validate another's pain, is as important here as in any therapeutic relationship.

Being partial also means acknowledging the unfairness of what has happened in a person's life. If empathy can be thought of as acknowledging a feeling, then being partial in this way might be thought of as the next step. First we recognize and acknowledge the depth of a patient's feeling and then we help the person to identify what was unfair in how he was treated. One of the important implications of thinking about fairness in relationships is that it gives us an opportunity to help people identify those times when they have received unfair treatment, the injustice to which they have been subjected in their own lives. Talking about fairness and unfairness often reminds people of former President Jimmy Carter's famous remark about the unfairness of life. Life is full of unfairness and the point of our focusing on it is not to deny this fact, or to say that life should be fair, but rather to recognize the unfairness and the lasting hurt that unfairness can sometimes cause.

In addition to being interested in the facts of each client's life circumstances, history, and individual psychological makeup, the contextual therapist has a particular interest in issues relevant to fairness. In attempting to be partial to each family member, the therapist may encounter situations in which it is difficult to side with a person's present behavior, for example, in the case of a parent who is being abusive or neglectful to young children. In such cases it is useful to explore the past injustices that led to the parent's inability to see the harm they are causing their children. This process allows the therapist to be partial to the person without endorsing his or her present actions.

Being partial involves more than being empathic and acknowledging the unfairness in a person's past. It also means helping people to give those they are close to (as well as themselves) credit for the efforts they have made to be helpful to others, to acknowledge their positive contributions to those who are most important to them. In couples and family work, being partial in this way also means that we will draw other family members' attention to those acts that deserve credit. We may do this in a general, open-ended manner by asking something like, "Do you see anything positive about the fact that your husband is willing to be straightforward with you about his concerns, despite the fact that you feel he is overly critical at times?" We may also call attention to possibilities for giving credit in a very focused and almost directive manner, "I don't know if you see it the same way that I do, but it seems to me that your daughter would like to be helpful to you and that she cares about you a great deal."

A fourth and essential aspect of being partial in a multidirected way involves helping people to see the impact of what they say and do on other people, especially those in their families. In contextual language, this aspect of multidirected partiality is often referred to as "holding people accountable." This can be the most difficult and challenging of the techniques we have discussed. It can also be the most crucial. Returning briefly to the couple mentioned above, we may ask the husband, "Is there anything to what your wife has said? Do you think you might be too critical at times?" In a session with a young adult and his mother, who was an active alcoholic during the young man's childhood but is no longer, we may ask, "Do you think that your son may have been hurt in some way that you did not intend during that time?" In asking this question we point out the imbalance in her relationship with her son; in holding her accountable for her actions we open a door for her to work toward greater balance, toward a more fair relationship. The goal here is not to criticize or humiliate, or to rearrange the family hierarchy or to shift the balance of power; it is rather to foster the growth of a more balanced relationship.

FROM PAST HURTS TO FUTURE POSSIBILITIES

Earlier in this chapter I talked about the problem of understanding how people who care about each other can still hurt each other or stand by while others are hurt. One's own pain is always much more real than another's pain. And if one's own pain is of sufficient magnitude and immediacy, then the pain of the other may not be real at all. It may be invisible. People who have been terribly hurt, especially during childhood, are particularly prone to this inability to see the distress of another person. If there was little caring or consideration to serve as a compensation or balm for their pain, then the risk of being insensitive to others' distress, even to the distress of their own children, spouses, or parents, is great. More than that, there is always the risk that such individuals will justify hurting others or be unmoved by the suffering of others based on their own past injuries.

From the contextual perspective, these people have accrued so much *destructive entitlement*, and rely on it so heavily, that they have become blind to the impact of their actions on others. This concept is both complex and central to the approach and so we shall return to it repeatedly.

But what is *destructive entitlement* and how could anyone possibly be entitled to be destructive? The term seems oxymoronic. Perhaps the clearest way to illustrate this apparent contradiction in terms is to consider a young child who has been diagnosed with a debilitating illness. There is no sense in which such a youngster can be said to have brought the illness on herself, no sense in which the youngster deserves the illness, no sense in which it is fair. On the other hand, it is clear that the youngster is entitled to some recompense for his or her suffering and loss, is entitled to have someone take responsibility for helping him deal with his anger, is entitled to a better life, and is entitled to be insensitive to the relatively minor misfortunes of others.

Some years ago a mother brought Dave, her 9-year-old son, to see me. Dave had sickle cell anemia, a chronic, life-threatening, genetically transmitted illness that causes frequent painful and frightening crises that often require hospitalization and transfusions. He was not referred to me for treatment of his illness, but because of his highly disruptive behavior at home and at school. He was hyperactive, impulsive, and inattentive in school. He was also physically aggressive both at home and in school. He had threatened to hit his sisters, his mother, and his father. He had also been suspended because he had threatened to hit his teachers and principal. He had also talked about wanting to die, and had tried to climb out a third floor window at school. His parents were completely distraught and his school had run out of ideas, plans, and options. When I first met Dave he was very angry; in our first meeting this little boy said, "I don't like this planet. It isn't fair." And of course he was absolutely right; he was *entitled* not to care about how his behavior might bother or inconvenience other people.

Reliance on destructive entitlement may be seen in a person's lack of sensitivity, caring, or concern for others; for their needs, feelings, hopes, and misfortunes. The person who relies on destructive entitlement is also particularly insensitive to the ways in which his or her actions affect others. Everybody occasionally does things that hurt others; this does not necessarily represent destructive entitlement, only human frailty. People who rely predominantly on destructive entitlement in relating to others, however, have experienced so much pain and injustice, that they have become blind to the harm that they cause others. A man who had been talking about his very painful and difficult childhood was asked if he hoped that things would be better for his children than they had been for him. The extent of his reliance on destructive entitlement was clear in his response, "Why should they?"

By way of contrast, we have all encountered people who have experienced great personal loss, personal injustice, and even personal tragedy in their lives and who are nonetheless able to be sensitive to others and to consider how their actions will effect other people. Examples of this sort of transcendence of personal tragedy are evident in all spheres of life. Among these are physicians and medical researchers who chose their fields in part due to early personal difficulties. I am thinking here of individuals who specialize in research on a disease process or in developing new treatments for a condition that might have led to the early death of their mother or father, or perhaps a condition from which they themselves suffer.

Organizations such as Mothers Against Drunk Driving or those advocating the control of handguns vividly reflect the ways in which some people are able to respond to personal tragedy in positive ways. These are people who typically express their motivation by saying that they are doing this work so that other families will not suffer as they have. All these individuals have certainly experienced injustice in their lives by anybody's standards. And so it is completely accurate to speak of these people as "having" much destructive entitlement. Like the youngster who suffered from sickle cell anemia, they have every right to be less than sensitive to other people's life difficulties. They have every right to be preoccupied with their own troubles. We would not be surprised if they were to rely on their destructive entitlement in dealing with other people. We would not be surprised if they were to use their own past hurts and injuries to justify being insensitive to others, perhaps even harmful to others. And yet these people are not insensitive to others. They are instead remarkably giving in their relationships with other people. Some of them have devoted their lives to helping others. These people have much accrued destructive entitlement but rely on its opposite, *constructive entitlement*, when it comes to their relationships and to all facets of their lives. Such people, those who seem invulnerable to the numbing and compassion-blocking effects of personal loss, have almost certainly had significant relational inoculations early in their lives. They may have had an especially nurturant and loving extended family who fostered their capacities to care about other people. Or there may have been one family member, a parent or perhaps a grandparent, whose guidance, protection, and care was sufficient to counterbalance difficulties and deprivations in childhood and later. For some people the invulnerability did not come from a biological family member, but from a close family friend, an honorary uncle or aunt.

People who can see the future as having possibilities not presented by the past are more likely to rely on constructive entitlement. These people, in contrast to those characterized by an inability to give to others, have preserved their capacity to care about others, to be considerate of others, to be sensitive to the pain of others, and above all to give to others. Where those characterized by reliance on destructive entitlement seem to be blocked in their capacity to give, these individuals seemed to have avoided these blockages. To borrow a term from Rotter (1954), these people appear to have greater "freedom of movement" with regard to their ability, their freedom, to give. The other group has a markedly constrained freedom to give. The hurt of the past has led them to give up that freedom. It has led them to replace the question "How can I enhance my own worth by being helpful to others?" with the worry "I have to think of myself first."

UNWILLING CARETAKING

One of the most dramatic and most frequent ways in which people are harmed is by being made into peoples' caretakers. This occurs earliest and with the most devastating consequences when young children are made the unwilling caretakers of their parents, but adults can also be made into unwilling caretakers of each other in their relationships. In the language of contextual therapy this state of unwillingly becoming a caretaker is referred to as *destructive parentification* or, more simply, *parentification*. Note that there is a distinction between the concept of a parental child as used by Minuchin (1974) and the destructive using of a child we are calling destructive parentification. Merely having some parent-like roles with regard to younger children does not necessarily constitute parentification in the sense in which we are using the term. A parentified person, whether child or adult, is called upon to act like a selflessly giving parent. In the case of a parentified child, this most often means that the child becomes the parent to his or her own parent. In a couple, the parentified person is put in a situation of explicitly or implicitly being required to care for the other as a parent would. Of course, all close relationships involve a measure of taking care of the other, but there is a dramatic difference between relationships in which this caretaking balances out over time and those in which one person does all the giving all the time.

ACKNOWLEDGING EFFORTS AND SACRIFICES

Earlier I mentioned the emphasis on helping people to acknowledge their own positive efforts and those of others as one of the defining features of this approach. Acknowledgment plays an important role from the first minute of the first session and takes several forms. When, in a first family session for example, a therapist asks whether a temporarily scapegoated person may have been trying to be helpful despite appearances, or whether this person may try to be helpful at other times, the therapist is really inviting other people in the family to acknowledge the person's positive efforts to give something of interpersonal value to them. The second form of acknowledgment involves acknowledging the injustice (unfairness) that has occurred in someone else's life. Examples would include both acknowledging how one's own actions have harmed another and acknowledging the unfairness of having been born with a disability or chronic life threatening illness. Acknowledging that another has been harmed, or that another has given generously, is one indicator of one's ability to act based on constructive rather than destructive entitlement.

People's most unpleasant, insensitive, inconsiderate, and angry statements and actions often reflect the imbalance in their lives: They have been hurt; they have been exploited; they have, they feel, tried to be helpful; and they have received no acknowledgment for either their pain or their good efforts from those closest to them. To a scapegoated person, one who has experienced only blame, acknowledgment from those who matter the most often has striking and salutary effects. A seemingly simple statement of appreciation for trying to help, or one of sympathy for struggling to overcome an injury, can literally make a world of difference; it is not unusual to see people's attitudes shift in a few moments from being aggressively confrontational to quietly receptive when they hear such acknowledgment from other family members.

A FIRST SESSION WITH A FAMILY

Many of the features of this way of working with individuals, couples, and families come into play in the first session. The following illustration highlights the emphasis on applying the principle of multidirected partiality and on looking for ways in which being hurt in the past can block a person's ability to be sensitive to and considerate of others. It also illustrates the important role played by acknowledgment. Finally, it touches on the way in which individual psychological issues are respected while maintaining an emphasis on helping people to focus on positives rather than on pathology. Later chapters will provide further discussion and illustration of these features of contextual work with families, with couples, and with individuals.

The Pear family consisted of 43-year-old Andrew; 39-year-old Jennifer, his wife; and their children Danny (11), Sue (8), and Stevie (8 months). Andrew and Jennifer called the therapist looking for help in dealing with what they described as Danny's "unmanageable" behaviors, including his restlessness at home and in school, his intense emotional reactions when he was frustrated, his very high level of activity, and his impulsivity.

The therapist began by asking about the problems with Danny. She did this because part of her responsibility as a clinician was to begin to formulate a diagnostic impression and to consider whether Danny might need a referral for medication, a neurological evaluation, or psychological testing to gain further information about cognitive strengths and weaknesses, learning style, or problems with attention and impulsivity. The therapist also realized that Andrew and Jennifer needed to know that as their therapist she took their complaints about Danny's behavior seriously and that she was interested in helping them to do something about them.

But the therapist did not want her need to evaluate Danny's psychological functioning to become the sole focus of therapy or even of the first session. And so after a very few minutes, she turned to Andrew and Jennifer and asked, "Despite the fact that Danny seems to get in trouble at school and does things at home that you wish he would not do, can you point to things that show you that he cares about you and that make you think he would like to be helpful to you and to the whole family?" Both Andrew and Jennifer said that when Danny was not "acting up" he could be "very sweet and considerate," especially with his baby brother, and that they had noticed and appreciated this. They also commented that he sometimes helped with various chores such as doing dishes or taking out the trash.

The therapist responded, "I'm glad to see that he is helpful at times. I was also wondering, though, if you have noticed any times when Danny was particularly sensitive to your feelings, to your moods, or if he seems to notice if you are upset or not feeling well?" Andrew said that he thought Danny was totally self-absorbed and did not think about anyone but himself. Jennifer said that her father had been very ill, that she was very worried about him and sometimes cried after speaking to her mother on the telephone. She added that her husband found it very difficult to respond to her upset feelings and so she rarely talked to him about these matters, but that Danny had come up to her and put his arm around her the last time that this had happened.

The therapist accomplished a number of goals by this series of questions. At the most obvious and superficial level, she began to draw Andrew's and Jennifer's attention to their son's positive behaviors. This gave her a way to open a door for

Jennifer and Andrew to acknowledge that their son had some important positive attributes, that he both wanted to be and was sensitive to others in his family. It also helped the therapist learn that Danny was possibly placed in a situation of taking care of his mother's emotional needs with regard to his grandfather's illness and was in this way being parentified. It was also very useful for her to see that Jennifer, despite her frustration with Danny and distress over her father's illness, was able to credit Danny's positive efforts. The therapist was especially heartened by Jennifer's ability to acknowledge Danny's parentification because she saw it as a first step toward addressing his anger.

The therapist had noticed that Andrew, on the other hand, seemed particularly angry with Danny. He interpreted his son's restlessness and impulsivity as being "disrespectful," something that he found very upsetting. As a way of beginning to understand this father's extreme anger with his little boy, the therapist asked, "What was it like when you were a child?" Andrew told the therapist that he was the third child in a family of seven, that he had received little in the way of attention or affection and that his parents' standards for behavior had been especially high and rigidly held. He added that he would not have dared to squirm in his seat at dinner or to interrupt an adult, for punishment would have been swift and severe.

He also added that no matter how hard he tried to earn good grades in school, something that was excruciatingly difficult for him, his father was never satisfied. Andrew made no effort to hide his lingering anger and resentment about these events of his childhood. The therapist let Andrew know that she understood and sympathized with him regarding his early difficulties, especially his own father's refusal to give him any credit for his efforts. She also gently raised this grandfather's side, anticipating later work toward *exoneration* (to be discussed in chapter 4) by asking Andrew, "Do you think that your father was so harsh and demanding because he was basically nasty or do you think that in his own way, however misguided, he may have felt he was helping you to achieve more in life by demanding more of you?"

The therapist could see that Andrew had been badly hurt as a young child, and that his continued preoccupation with the unfairness of his early life made it hard for him to see his son in a positive light or to be sympathetic to him. She hoped that being acknowledged for having been parentified himself would free Andrew of the need to justify his self-concern by reference to this history of exploitation and enable him to respond more sensitively and with greater consideration to his son. It would not be far off to say that up to this point Andrew had been justifying his harsh behavior in the present on the grounds that he had been badly hurt himself. In the language of contextual therapy Andrew's continued *reliance on destructive entitlement* could be seen in his blindness to his child's developmental and interpersonal needs and in his blindness to the positives about his child.

Andrew's comments, combined with what seemed to be an overreaction to his son's behavior, raised questions about the extent to which his experiences as a child were coloring his perceptions of his own children. They also raised questions about his ability to understand his son's behaviors apart from their impact on him. From the perspective of Andrew's psychological functioning, then, the question of narcissism emerged, especially with regard to its possible impact on the family and on the father-son relationship.

Andrew's remarks also alerted the therapist to the role that *loyalty* issues (to be discussed in greater detail in chapter 4) might play in what superficially appeared as Andrew's insensitivity. She began to be interested in the possibility that Andrew might experience himself as being disloyal were he to be a more considerate, giving, and acknowledging parent than his own father was. While seeming to reject his father as a parent, perhaps even as a person, in some ways he acted toward Danny as his father had toward him, in part perhaps continuing to be *invisibly loyal.*

The therapist noted all this and yet maintained her emphasis on trying to see each family member's side and on helping them to find opportunities for acknowledgment. She then began to ask Jennifer about her family in a similar manner. Throughout this history taking the therapist was particularly alert to those early experiences that had hurt Jennifer in ways that might have made it difficult for her to be aware of the burden she might be placing on her son in confiding her emotional distress to him. In the language of this approach, the therapist listened for early experiences of *unfairness* that might have led Jennifer to rely on *destructive entitlement* in her interactions with other people in the family.

As a way to wrap up the first session, the therapist asked Andrew and Jennifer if they could see any connections between their histories and their present concerns. They replied that they had never thought about it but that there might be. The therapist then shared her impression that both of them had had more than their fair share of difficulties in childhood and asked if they hoped for a better life for their children. They said that they did and that this was their reason for coming for therapy; this single statement, reflecting Andrew and Jennifer's commitment to helping their children, left the therapist feeling very optimistic about the eventual outcome of therapy.

2

MULTIDIRECTED PARTIALITY

Our study of how to put the principle of multidirected partiality to work continues with illustrative therapy sessions with adults and their young or adolescent children. These sessions provide the richest and most dramatic illustrations of what can be done to work actively on behalf of each person who is likely to be affected by the process of therapy. When we can actually sit down with members of two or more generations we may directly learn about how people have been hurt in the past, how they are trying to consider each other's needs today, and how they may be even more considerate in the future. We are also able to hold each of these people accountable for their actions and the ways in which these actions have affected or are likely to affect others. As we shall see, experience in talking with grandparents, parents, and children is invaluable when our attention turns to working with a couple or a single adult.

A MATTER OF BALANCE

Before launching into the specifics of how we may understand, appreciate, acknowledge, and even confront each of the people whom our work may affect, let's reflect on why the techniques associated with multidirected partiality are emphasized as much as they are. This leads back to the question of what contextual therapy is all about, and what its fundamental goals are. All theories of personality and most, if not all, models of therapy are built on the premise that the quality of one's interpersonal relationships reflects the quality of one's inner psychological functioning. We add to this the observation that people benefit from relationships in which there is a fair balance between giving and receiving. People's emotional and psychological well-being, their experience of their own value as human beings, is linked to both their sense of their own contributions to others and their actual contributions to others. The emphasis on the psychological benefits of thinking about how we can help others is far from unique. To cite just one prominent example, Alfred Adler, a Viennese physician and contemporary of Freud's, made the concept of *gemeinschaftsgefühle*, feeling for the community, the cornerstone of his *individual psychology* (1923, 1924, 1927). Adler felt that many adjustment problems could be traced to a relative absence of community feeling, to a difficulty in considering how one might benefit others by one's actions. Much of contextual therapy is based on two closely related observations. Those who undervalue their ability to give, or who feel that others undervalue it, may experience self-doubt, low self-esteem, depression, and related psychological distress. Those who feel that they are giving too much are often chronically angry, and seen by others as self-focused and over-entitled.

Traditional healing ceremonies of the Navajo people of the American Southwest are built on the premise that emotional or behavioral disturbances are signs of disharmony between man or woman and nature. During these rituals the Navajo healer guides a process that, with the participation of the community, brings the disturbed person back into harmony with nature. Restoring people to harmony is the primary concern. Changing behavior, what we might call symptom relief, is secondary, and is expected to follow the reestablishment of harmonious balance.

The essence of this therapy is analogous; we aim to help people achieve balance, a kind of harmony, in their closest and most important relationships. Those who lack the strength to state their own side, to stake a claim and defend it, even when by any objective standards they are in the right, are helped to shift toward being more willing to ask for what they want, perhaps to demanding it, and to accepting from others. Those who are unable to appreciate other people's experiences, feelings, and needs, those who lack consideration for others, are helped along the path of greater sensitivity to others. In the technical language of contextual therapy, the former are people who have earned constructive entitlement but who do not, for whatever reasons, *feel* entitled to ask for what they want or need from others. As a consequence, they are likely to feel both deprived and resentful. The latter, those who worry, "I have to think of myself first because no one else will," rely on destructive entitlement in relating to others.

OPPORTUNITIES FOR INCREASING SELF-WORTH

The issue is whether one builds one's life on looking for opportunities to enhance one's self-worth by contributing to others or whether one spends one's time preoccupied by anxiety over whether anyone will care. And this is where the principle of multidirected partiality comes in, where, if you will, the therapy comes in. We intentionally emphasize the feature of *reliance* when we speak of the person who *relies* on destructive entitlement. This is because the person does not merely *have* destructive entitlement, he actually does rely on it in almost every aspect of his life. He uses his destructive entitlement to energize, to motivate, and to justify his actions. Perhaps he grew up during the great depression and now constantly worries about money. Perhaps he felt materially or emotionally deprived as a child and is now self-indulgent and self-centered to the point of depriving his own children in the same way that he was.

Some may be wondering if all this talk about reliance on destructive entitlement is superfluous. Why can we not be content to observe that this individual is highly narcissistic and leave it at that? The answer to this very reasonable question highlights several key features of the contextual approach. This person's narcissism is clearly an important aspect of his psychological functioning, as are issues of anxiety and depression, both of which may be present as well. As we noted at the beginning of chapter 1, we attend to each person's personality organization just as we do other issues of individual psychological functioning. When speaking formally, these are considered as aspects of dimension II (individual psychology).

This leads to the other issue raised by the question of narcissism. How does this person's narcissism affect those with whom he is, or might be, in close relationship? How can we help this person to be more considerate of others, and by so doing build up his self-worth and self-esteem? If we can help this man to identify how he has been hurt in the past; if we can find ways to acknowledge this past hurt; if we can help him to see the impact of his actions on others; if we can help him to see opportunities to move beyond his anxiety-driven concern for himself; if we can help him to begin to be interested in how he might be helpful to others, then perhaps we may be able to facilitate a process of beginning to move toward relying on constructive entitlement rather than on destructive entitlement.

GIVING TOO MUCH

Let's turn for a moment to people who cannot say "no," people who always put themselves, their feelings, and their needs last. In contrast to the "overentitled" individual, these people cannot recognize what they have earned. The overentitled person cannot see anyone else's side of things. These people cannot see their own sides, cannot see what *they* are entitled to. The overentitled person is unwilling to give others what they request regardless of the merit of the request; this person *overgives*, to the point of denying his own wishes, and to the point of building up considerable resentment.

This self-denial, overgiving, and resentment may become a life style. The issue is not one of assertiveness per se. Although some of these people may have difficulties in being assertive, others are very comfortable being assertive on someone else's behalf. Instruction in how to be assertive is of only very limited usefulness in such cases. Their problems with assertiveness only arise when the situation requires being assertive on their own behalf. Instead of staking claims for the things to which they are entitled based on what they have contributed in the past, these people may only be able to make demands based on their anger and resentment. Instead of, "Having contributed so much I feel it fair that I ask for something," they may feel, "I've given and given to everybody; I'm mad as hell and I'm just going to think about myself now." It is as if they need to point to their overgiving as a sign that others have taken advantage of them, justifying their claims by emphasizing how they have been hurt and exploited in the past. The person who gives too much, like the person who refuses to give, uses his or her anger and resentment to justify making a claim; he or she also relies on destructive entitlement.

Both of these stereotypes, and they are of course stereotypes, represent people whose relationships are out of balance. Some refuse to consider other people's experiences, refuse to be sensitive to how they have hurt or are hurting other people, and refuse to give except on their own terms. The others give, but only because they feel relatively undeserving themselves; they give in such a way that the long-term result is anger and resentment. Recipients of their largesse are ultimately made to pay for it, perhaps several times over.

If people benefit from being in relationships in which there is a balance over time between what they do for others and what they receive from others, then our job is to foster movement in this direction. For both of the stereotypical groups we have looked at, as well as for others, this means helping people to move toward the position of asking the question posed in the previous chapter, "How can I increase my own feelings of worth and value by contributing to others in ways that make sense to me?" How can I rely more on constructive entitlement and less on destructive entitlement? For the overgiving person the emphasis will be on giving in ways that are congruent with their own self-image, their strengths, their capacities; on giving spontaneously because they can and want to, not because they are forced to or lack the self-respect to refuse any request. This is why we acknowledge people's positive contributions as well as their pain and injuries: to try to help people carefully identify how they have been helpful to others, as well as how they have been harmed and exploited; to help them ask those closest to them for acknowledgment of their contributions and apologies for their injuries; and above all to help people become increasingly free to acknowledge each other's efforts, to give to each other.

PRESENTING OPTIONS

Just as people can more easily quit smoking if offered a benign substitute, so people can more easily decrease their reliance on destructive entitlement if they have another option. A woman who justifies being harsh to her children, critical of her husband, devious with her colleagues, and unforgiving of her subordinates on the grounds that she suffered and was deprived early in life will not respond well to being told that she did not really suffer all that much. After all, she has in a very real sense been energized by that suffering. She has relied on her anger and sense of entitlement as she has negotiated on her own behalf with family as well as with coworkers. "My self-concern, my insensitivity, my lack of consideration for you is nothing compared to what was done to me, is nothing compared to how I was hurt, as a child, as a young woman, and last week. I am entitled to put myself first *and* last, justified in hurting you just a little if it helps me enough." If this is the only way that she knows to get what she wants out of life, and if we try to disrupt her world view by discounting the validity of her anger, she will rightly feel that we are taking something from her. This is what we mean by "reliance on destructive entitlement." She is likely to be much more interested in thinking about how she might be able to be less critical and more considerate of her children or her husband if we first acknowledge her legitimate pain and anger about her suffering, and especially if we, and later her family, can acknowledge her efforts to be helpful to her family. Perhaps she feels that working hard, advancing professionally, and earning a good salary are the most important and generous things she can do, far more important than day-to-day sensitivity regarding the mundane realities of life. Giving a higher priority to someone else's needs may entail a loss of her only way to claim anything for herself. As long as this is true, her capacity to give to others will be, to a greater or lesser extent, blocked. Acknowledgment from the therapist, especially if it leads to acknowledgment from the people closest to her, can go a long way toward removing that block. This in turn will help her to be free to give to others; then she will be able to claim what she wants and needs based on what she has contributed, not what she has suffered.

SPONTANEOUS GIVING

We assume that a desire to give to others and to be helpful to others is a more natural condition than its opposite. Being free to give spontaneously reflects an underlying trust that somehow, in some way, things will balance out over time, that what is given will be returned or compensated. There is no more lucid image of this than the spontaneous generosity of a very young child. Anyone who has spent time around young children is well aware of this. Very young children freely express distress by crying. They are equally free in expressing affection and the need for affection by climbing into a parent's lap without inhibition. They equally freely give of themselves. They will take a Cheerio from their bowl and place it in the mouth of their mother, or perhaps try to feed it to a plush animal toy. They will freely and spontaneously kiss and hug the family pet, their older brother or sister, and their parents and grandparents. They will crawl up into any available and friendly lap.

This spontaneity reflects a basic trust (Erikson, 1963) in the reliability of the world. Some gradual decrease in this spontaneity is of course natural. Maturity requires some reserve; spontaneously kissing strangers and casual acquaintances is the norm in very few places—Hollywood perhaps, or Cannes. On the other hand, some people are able to retain their ability to spontaneously be helpful to other people, while some seem to lose it.

What happens to interfere with this freedom to give and to demand and accept giving from others? The first chapter provided a partial answer to this question in its discussion of destructive entitlement. People who have been repeatedly injured in childhood in ways that damage their basic trust in the world, and especially in their parents, begin to lose their capacity to give spontaneously to others. They may also lose the capacity to ask for what they need and in fact to ask for what they deserve. The fundamental goal in all of this work is to facilitate people's growth as individuals and as participants in relationships. In other words, our efforts in being partial to people are directed toward helping them to be more attuned to thinking about what is fair with regard to both their own needs *and* to those of others. To be a bit more theoretical for a moment, we hope to help people increase their self-worth, their belief in that self-worth, and in their capacity for spontaneous giving and receiving.

The first session with the Pear family held several illustrations of how a therapist can be partial to each person in a family. The therapist was able to help Jennifer and Andrew surface their concerns while taking 11-year-old Danny's side as well. Later, in raising the possibility that Andrew's father may have had some redeeming characteristics, she was actively considerate of a person she will, in all likelihood, never meet. This emphasis on considering everyone's perspective and being willing to actively side with the person who requires this the most at a particular time, has a number of practical implications for the way in which therapy is conducted.

SOWING SEEDS AND OPENING DOORS

As a general rule, the contextual approach is more likely to look at therapy as a catalyzing process, as one that plants seeds and helps them to grow, rather than one that directly manipulates people's interpersonal relationships. As we look at cases in detail, and especially the case of the S family in the final chapters, we shall see that it is possible to give room to people to spontaneously be more considerate in their actions, and to be more responsible as well, without tieing one's hands behind one's back, and without being a passive therapist. The process of opening doors and windows for people may lead to pointing out where the doors are and how the light from the window illuminates relationships. So we open the doors and windows; we talk about what lies beyond the doors and how the light may permit a clearer understanding of a situation or problem if one stands by the window. We may go so far as taking their hand and walking them to the door. We may go to the door ourselves and describe what we see.

We may even tell our patients what others have seen and done on the other side of the doorway, and in some situations what we have done ourselves on the other side of the doorway. But only in the most exceptional circumstance will we try to push them through to the other side. We provide the greatest opportunities for people to grow if we provide a general direction without too much restriction. If people need greater structure, we provide it, but only gradually, sharpening the focus bit by bit. For example we may ask a man who is fuming that his wife "made" him participate in therapy if he can see anything positive in her motivation for making the appointment and pushing him to come to it. If his response is negative, we may return to the topic a bit later, asking if she deserves credit for taking a strong stand for the marriage and for being willing to stick to what she believes in despite his bluster.

A related and extremely important implication of focusing on being fair to each and every person who will be affected by the therapy is that each person is important; each deserves to be taken seriously. This means that the therapist will invite each person (in family sessions this includes children of all ages) to respond to questions or to make comments. It means that the therapist will ask children and others to clarify remarks that were spoken softly and that would otherwise have been ignored. And it also means that the therapist will not smile or laugh when a young child or one struggling with a speech difficulty struggles to express herself, even if her parents do so. In the context of a therapy demonstration it also means that the therapist will caution the audience against this as well.

DIAGNOSIS

The issue of diagnosis also provides opportunities to apply the principle of multidirected partiality. It also provides limitless opportunities for scapegoating. In some instances we may be most considerate by refusing to diagnosis, as I did when an enraged ex-husband insisted that his son's enuresis was caused by his ex-wife's "mental illness," a label he insisted I give her. Less in the realm of high drama, but more in the realm of everyday practice, I regularly choose not to diagnose highly energetic, independent-minded, and adventuresome four-year-old boys as "hyperactive" without a great deal of evidence of an underlying neurological problem.

On the other hand, a diagnosis can sometimes provide a

source of relief and an antidote to scapegoating. A middle-aged man who has felt that there was something wrong for many years, who has perhaps been perplexed by his irritability and lack of energy, may feel relieved to hear that he has been depressed and that there is something to do about it. Parents who have felt guilty and helpless for many years because their seven-year-old is always in trouble in school and never seems to have any friends may experience relief to learn that his difficulties reflect a subtle developmental disorder for which help is available.

Being willing to be partial to each family member can require some fancy footwork. There will be times when adults present their child to the therapist as the root of all the family's difficulties and as the putative "patient" not because he is suffering but because he is "making everybody else miserable." We would all like to be able to swoop in and put a stop to this scapegoating and parentification. But trying to do so with too much vigor may be more than the parents can tolerate, and so we may need to temporarily parentify the child ourselves so that we will have the opportunity to help him later. This does not mean that we join in the scapegoating. It does mean, however, that we may have to temper the degree to which we help him to raise his side, especially if our initial efforts to do so meet with fierce reactions.

ACKNOWLEDGING PARENTIFICATION: THREE CASES

Ten-year-old Mark and his parents met with their therapist the morning after he had been suspended for swearing at his teacher. After a brief discussion of the incident leading up to the suspension, Mark's father began to talk about his conflicts regarding discipline.

FATHER: I go back and forth when things like this happen. I can't stand it when he gets in trouble; I mean I'm practically on a first name basis with the principal. But I want to support my son too. He hasn't had it so easy all the time. I used to have quite a temper, and my wife and I were separated for a while there. I know that was rough for him.

THERAPIST: May I ask Mark about this?

Although this question may appear unnecessary, it serves several important functions. First, it underlines the primary role of the parent relative to the therapist in all matters pertaining to the child. Second, it provides explicit permission not only for therapist to ask the question, but for the child to respond freely and openly.

MARK: I remember one Christmas when I was little. I went downstairs to see if Santa Claus was real and I saw them yelling and fighting, and my mom ran out of the house.

THERAPIST: I'd like to ask Mark's mother about this. From your perspective, would this fit with what your husband has said about things having been rough for Mark? [*The therapist provides an opportunity for Mark's mother to acknowledge the unfairness of his early life.*]

MOTHER: Yes, just that sort of thing. And Mark had a lot of responsibility for his brothers when we were separated and I was alone with them.

MARK: I had to watch them when she was working and if something happened I couldn't always get her on the telephone.

THERAPIST: How old was Mark then?

MOTHER: He was about seven.

THERAPIST: As you think about that now, does it seem like that may have been a lot for a child to take on? [*The therapist invites Mark's mother to acknowledge how he was parentified.*]

MOTHER: It really was.

FATHER: There's no question about it.

THERAPIST: As I listen to Mark he seems angry about these events. Does it seem that way to you as well?

The therapist raises the issue of anger, not because emotional expression or catharsis is an end in itself, but to provide an opportunity for Mark's parents to acknowledge that he experienced great unfairness and deserves both an apology and help in overcoming the lasting effects of those difficult early years. Mark's anger is a manifestation of his past and present parentification, of the imbalance in his relationship with other family members; he has been required to give much and yet has received little in the way of acknowledgment or help. The therapist's goal here is to catalyze both; to make it easier for Mark's parents to acknowledge that too much was asked of Mark as a young child and to point out the need for helping him now. If Mark's parents can do this and strongly acknowledge his efforts to help the family he will not have to continue to show them how unfairly he was treated by being angry and defiant; he will not need to rely so heavily on destructive entitlement.

FATHER: Yes, and I guess I don't really blame him. But at the same time I try to tell him you can't stay in the past. You've got to go on. I do feel badly for him. I guess you could say I feel guilty, but it's getting to be too much to take.

THERAPIST: It sounds like one problem now is how to let Mark know that you care and feel badly about his being hurt before, that you understand that he may still be angry about it; how to do that and yet hold the line regarding his behavior in school. [*The therapist endeavors to see the predicament that Mark's parents face.*]

As is evident from this brief excerpt, Mark's parents were able, when asked, to consider their son as a unique person and to acknowledge how the events and circumstances that had hurt him early in his childhood might well be important in understanding his presently unacceptable behaviors in school. In some families, however, one or both parents have been so badly hurt themselves that they have great difficulty in seeing their child's side at first.

The next case illustrates this sort of situation. It also illustrates the way in which a therapist may move beyond openended questions to quite definitive statements in being partial to one person. Fourteen-year-old Michelle had been admitted to the adolescent unit of a psychiatric hospital by her mother. She had made numerous suicidal statements, and had intense, albeit sporadic, episodes of rage during which she had threatened to hurt her mother as well as herself. As the family evaluation began, Michelle's mother initially appeared to be remarkably insensitive to her daughter's distress. She said that her daughter had always been difficult and had "just gotten worse" as she entered adolescence. She also said that the big problems had begun during the previous year when Michelle had frequently refused to go to school, a problem that had escalated recently. She made such comments as, "She's just being manipulative. This is all just a big act to get her own way."

Despite her best efforts to be partial to Michelle's mother, the therapist could see little to credit in her present behavior or actions. Hoping to learn something about this woman's past that would provide the basis for building a trustworthy relationship, something to which she could be could be partial, the therapist asked, "What was it like when you were growing up?" This is a useful technique in working with anyone whose present actions manifest little sensitivity to or consideration for others. The technique, which basically involves learning about the ways in which the person has been hurt in the past, is equally useful in sessions with couples, with individuals, or as we see here, with families.

In this session, and in response to the therapist's interest in her earlier years, Michelle's mother began to talk about her own very difficult personal and family history. Many members of her family had experienced severe depression. Several, including her own mother, had made suicide attempts. Michelle's father had died suddenly of a cerebral aneurism when Michelle was 12 years old. Michelle's mother herself had struggled with depression since her teens, a problem that had been particularly severe during the years immediately following her husband's death. Having heard this, the therapist was able to acknowledge the unfairness and hurt in Michelle's mother's life, something she needed before she could in turn acknowledge her daughter's suffering.

THERAPIST: You've had a lot of pain in your life.

MOTHER: I've had my share.

THERAPIST: And had you hoped that things would be better for your daughter than they were for you?

MOTHER: I've always done my best, but she never appreciates it. All I get in return is her mouth and her attitude. I stayed up until one in the morning ironing an outfit for school, and with my back problems I can tell you it was not easy. And what did I get or for my trouble? Michelle refused to wear what I had picked out for her. She just threw them right down on the floor. [*At this point Michelle is sitting silently, staring defiantly at her mother. She has so far refused to say anything.*]

THERAPIST: You have done a lot, perhaps more than was done for you.

The therapist acknowledges both mother's positive contributions and her past deprivations. In doing so the therapist's goal is that Michelle's mother may be a little better able to do the same for Michelle; to acknowledge her positive efforts and her difficulties.

MOTHER: That's for sure. There was nobody to iron for me. I had to do it for myself.

THERAPIST: You hoped that after putting yourself out for Michelle, after staying up so late, especially with your back bothering you—had hoped that she would show some appreciation. [*The therapist again acknowledges mother's efforts to do something for her daughter and her anger at not being given any credit for this.*]

MOTHER: It would have been nice. But all I got instead was a lot of mouth.

THERAPIST: The mouthiness, refusing to go to school, the threats, and now talking about hurting herself, and even hurting you. Despite all these troubling behaviors, is there anything you can point to in what Michelle does or says that makes you think that she would like to help you?

MOTHER: If she wanted to help she would go to school and stop screaming and carrying on whenever I ask her to do anything.

THERAPIST: Her refusing to go to school really gets to you.

MOTHER: She gets good grades. Or she did anyway when she used to go to school. *I* had trouble in school, but I went.

THERAPIST: So it bothers you more that she could do well, that perhaps she could do more than you were able to.

MOTHER: I just don't understand why she won't go to school. It's driving me crazy.

THERAPIST: You had said that you've been depressed.

MOTHER: Wouldn't you be depressed if your kid acted like this?

THERAPIST: Despite all her unpleasant behavior, does Michelle notice when you are depressed or lonely?

Michelle has been parentified. This question is intended to do two things: To assess mother's level of awareness of this, and to prepare for the discussion of Michelle's concern for and efforts to help her mother that follows.

MOTHER: I think so.

THERAPIST: I would like to ask you a question that may sound crazy to you, but I would like to ask it anyway.

MOTHER: Okay.

THERAPIST: Do you think it's possible that, along with all the adolescent acting up, Michelle is worried about you? You had said that you were always very close when she was younger. Do you think she may be afraid that something might happen to you when she is at school? [*As the therapist asks this "crazy question" there is a shift in Michelle's attitude. She quite sud-*

denly is no longer sullen, but rather listening intently and watching her mother's response.]

MOTHER: No, she just doesn't want to go to school.

THERAPIST: You know, I don't want to get into an argument with you but I think that this is a point where you and I see things differently. Let me tell you what I mean. When we were talking I noticed how Michelle was paying close attention. I do think that she cares about you, that she would like to be helpful to you. It would be hard for a young person to know what to do though. Maybe staying home from school to be with you is the only thing she can think of.

The therapist asks Michelle's mother to consider the implications of what she has said: that she is depressed, that Michelle is aware of this, and yet that she is sure that Michelle could not possibly be staying home to watch over her. In other words, the therapist is holding her accountable for what she has said.

The next illustration is drawn from a case in which 13-year-old Janet said during a therapy session that her stepfather had asked her to sit on his lap, a request that had made her very uncomfortable. She said he had stopped making such requests when she protested, but that she still felt uncomfortable about it. The therapist wanted to address the issue in a way that would ensure that Janet was not put in similar awkward situations in the future, but without parentifying her by using her to be heavily judgmental of her stepfather. We join the session about one third of the way through.

STEPFATHER: It's very difficult to know how to act with Janet. I know how to get close to my other kids (sons aged 7 and 9 and a 3-year-old daughter from his previous marriage), but I just don't know how to be a parent to a teenage daughter.

THERAPIST: It is difficult. It's difficult for any man, any father, whether a natural father, an adoptive father, or a stepfather, to know how to be close with a daughter. Especially after they reach a certain age, it's always sort of awkward to know how to express affection, how to find the right way. With girls like Janet, well they're really not little girls; they are beginning to be young women, and there can be a very natural discomfort for both the father and the daughter.

The therapist takes both Janet's and her stepfather's situations into consideration. She brings up the issue of appropriate boundaries between father and daughter, holding Janet's stepfather accountable for his behavior, but in a way that recognizes his wish to be a good parent and his confusion about how to do so. Of course, such a moderate response is only possible because his transgression, while significant, is relatively minor.

STEPFATHER: [*Nodding*] I just don't know what I'm supposed to do. It's a lot easier to know what to do with my own little girl.

THERAPIST: It's a whole lot easier to know how to be affectionate with a little girl, a three- or four-year-old, who wants to sit on your lap and be hugged. It's much more difficult when your little girl becomes a teenager.

STEPFATHER: It is. I just don't know what to do.

MOTHER: Sometimes he'll be going out to a store or somewhere and he'll ask Janet if she wants to go along, but she always says no.

THERAPIST: When you were Janet's age, did you do a lot of things with your father?

MOTHER: I wish I could have. My father died when I was only 9. And before that he seemed to be working most of the time, but I loved it when he did take me places with him. I'd like Janet to have that with my husband, especially since her real father is so far away and she hardly ever sees him.

THERAPIST: So you really want Janet to have the kind of closeness with your husband that you missed out on with your own father?

This is a clear example of parentification in that Janet's mother is trying to salve her own wounds by pushing Janet into an artificial and forced intimacy with her stepfather. Instead of confronting this as bad parenting, however, the therapist follows the principle of multidirected partiality and acknowledges this mother's loss and pain, just as she earlier took Janet's side by talking with her stepfather about appropriate and inappropriate behaviors.

FAMILY THERAPY VS. INDIVIDUAL THERAPY: A MEANINGFUL DISTINCTION?

Another way in which we can be partial is by offering an opportunity to talk about concerns privately. This can be a useful procedure in working with parents and children as well as in working with couples. It may, however, raise some conceptual as well as technical questions for those who are accustomed to thinking of contextual therapy as just another form of family therapy. And it would be surprising if many people did not think of the approach in just that way: as one of many variants of family therapy. After all, chapters on contextual therapy appear in each of the two editions of the *Handbook of Family Therapy* (Gurman & Kniskern, 1981, 1991). Those who identify themselves as contextual therapists are likely to be members of the American Association for Marriage and Family Therapy (AAMFT), the American Family Therapy Academy (AFTA), the Division of Family Psychology of the American Psychological Association, and similar organizations. Ivan Boszormenyi-Nagy, the founder of the contextual approach, has been honored by the American Association for Marriage and Family Therapy, the American Family Therapy Academy, and other "family therapy" organizations. Articles discussing various aspects of the approach appear in *The Journal of Marriage and Family Therapy* and similar publications.

Early in the history of family therapy the idea of meeting with whole families, initially psychotic adults and their parents, was so radical that the definition of family therapy as a field tended to focus on this dramatic difference from the then dominant psychoanalytic approaches. Many early practitioners of family therapy had originally been trained in psychoanalysis and wished to break sharply from and emphasize their differences from that tradition. One way of doing this was to highlight the conjoint nature of family therapy. From this perspective, "family therapies" were typically considered to be those that involved meetings or sessions in which families, parents, children, and perhaps grandparents and other relatives participated together. Some early family therapists also chose to ignore differences among individuals, especially differences in psychological strengths and weaknesses, focusing instead on patterns of family communication, power, and structure.

Early practitioners of these approaches were so committed to family systems ideas that they sometimes engaged in procedures that may seem silly in retrospect. For example, it was not uncommon for some of these first generation family therapists and their trainees to refuse to talk on the telephone with any family member, no matter how urgent the concern, or to refuse to meet with the family if one person was unable to participate in the session, no matter what the reason. At the height of "systemic chic" an otherwise sensible therapist might well have thought it reasonable to send a family home without seeing them because one person who had been present the week before, say an uncle or grandparent, had decided to skip that session; such a decision would typically have been based on a belief that the whole family "needed" that person to be absent.

The early emphasis on "systemic purity" is much less prevalent today, as is the notion that one must vigorously patrol the boundary between family therapy and individual therapy. But belief that such a distinction has meaning is very much alive and is often a source of confusion and inefficiency. Any experienced clinician can recount instances in which a couple had a "marital therapist"; one or both spouses, an "individual therapist"; and the family, a "family therapist." If one of the family members received medication, and if none of the therapists was a medical doctor, there may also have been a psychiatrist involved. A cynic may suggest that such arrangements serve only the financial interests of the practitioners. And yet they often reflect the sincere belief that one cannot provide support, understanding, encouragement, or a trustworthy relationship to a patient *and* to his or her spouse, children, siblings, or parents.

At one time agencies serving children and their families typically assigned one worker (often a child psychiatrist or child psychologist) to the child and another worker (usually a social worker) to the parent (i.e., mother). Times have changed, disciplinary lines have blurred in healthy and productive ways, and most of these agencies have adopted family therapy as an accepted modality of treatment. And yet one still hears earnest debates about whether or not a therapist will be compromising the quality of his relationship with a child if he "sees" the child in both family and individual sessions. As in the case of adults and their families, the underlying assumption is that a therapist is only able to side with one person or group of people; either with the child or the parents, but not with both. Interestingly, this question often troubles family therapists as much as it does those who identify themselves as child therapists. Multidirected partiality provides a way to help each person involved in therapy articulate his or her needs, experiences, regrets, and past hurts, thus providing a means of accomplishing a task faced by all clinicians who work with young children: All clinicians, whether they identify themselves as family therapists, social workers, child psychologists, or child psychiatrists, must find ways to be helpful to a child's parents if they are to truly help the child.

One of the advantages of the contextual approach is that it avoids the problems inherent in throwing the baby out with the bath water. Like the systemic family therapists, and their psychodynamic predecessors such as Alfred Adler and Harry Stack Sullivan, we place great importance on what happens among people, on the interpersonal aspect of life. We are also concerned, however, with individual people, with their pain, their experiences, and their thoughts. We also find great benefit in regularly offering individual sessions to those we work with as part of a couple or a family. The central principle of multidirected partiality directs therapists to consider the impact of their actions on all those who may be affected by what happens in therapy; it does not require that all those people be in the room with the therapist.

Bearing all of this in mind, one of the ways we endeavor to be partial is to offer each person an opportunity for one or more private sessions with the therapist. From a clinical as well as an ethical and legal perspective, it is always a good idea to spell out the limits of privacy before meeting with an individual in such circumstances. These should go well beyond the usual child protective and Tarasoff-related duty to warn issues that apply to all clinical work. With some couples, for example, one may wish to have a clear understanding that individual meetings are private but that the therapist reserves the right to reveal any information that one spouse tells her if she feels that keeping such a "secret" would compromise the therapy. For example a man may tell the therapist that he is having an affair and is actively planning to leave the marriage. While a therapist may or may not wish to reveal this information, a frank discussion of the limits of privacy beforehand will give her the freedom to do this if she feels it to be required. When working with adolescents, I inform both the adolescent and his or her parents that an individual meeting will be private except for information that leads me to believe there is a current bodily risk to either the adolescent or someone else. I also inform the adolescent, however, that I may suggest he share some of the things we talk about with his parents if I feel it will be clinically helpful, but that I will not do so myself without his permission.

The situation is somewhat different with preadolescent and younger children. Where a 15-year-old may benefit from an individual session or two, and a 17-year-old may have a great deal to talk about privately, I rarely spend more than 20 or 30 minutes individually with a 9- or 10-year-old before suggesting that it may be a good idea to talk with her parents about the issues we have been discussing. As with the adolescents, I do give the child the right to veto any planned revelations, but have only once had a child take advantage of this opportunity. This was a 7-year-old boy who was adamant in his refusal to reveal to his mother that he had developed a fondness for the girl who sat next to him in class. Often, however, children embrace the opportunity to have someone help them talk with their parents about their concerns, their fears, their anxieties, and their wishes.

THERAPY FOR FAMILIES

Contextual therapy is more accurately thought of as therapy *for* families than as "family therapy." Just as family physicians make themselves available to help all family members, so too do we. The notion of being the therapist for an adult, a couple, their children, and for the family as a whole may take clinicians some time to get used to. Patients and their families, however, seem to find this a sensible and intuitively appealing arrangement. Even those involved as gatekeepers in managed care organizations often appreciate the efficiency made possible by communicating with one clinician instead of several.

Therapy with the Pear family illustrates how individual and family sessions may be interwoven. Following the first session with the Pear family (chapter 1), the therapist invited both Andrew and Jennifer to meet with her individually if they wished. She made this offer not because she thought that they harbored secrets from each other, but because she wanted to offer her undivided attention, her support, and her encouragement to each person to discuss difficult issues in future combined sessions. In working with couples especially, one frequently finds that each partner is most reluctant to bring up just those issues upon which the future of the relationship may hinge. People sometimes worry that their partner will steamroller over them, discounting the importance and legitimacy of their concerns. They equally often voice concern that it would hurt their partner too much if they were honest either about what had hurt them in the relationship in the past or about their needs in the present. Individual meetings with the therapist can be quite helpful in addressing both of these kinds of concerns. The therapist can help the person prepare to state his or her side of a difficult situation, simultaneously holding the person accountable for the impact on his or her partner of doing so. A related reason for offering individual sessions is to give each person an opportunity to talk about parents and siblings without feeling disloyal to them.

Jennifer Pear asked for an appointment later that same week; Andrew said he would be very busy but that he might be able to leave work early sometime in the next two weeks and that he would call to arrange an appointment.

The therapist thought about pushing the issue but decided to hold off in order to give Andrew some room to make up his own mind. This emphasis on providing opportunities rather than directing people is an essential feature of the approach and is consistent with the aim of facilitating spontaneous actions, not coerced ones. If the therapist had pushed Andrew into an individual session, and if it had been helpful it would have been the therapist, not Andrew, who would have made the more significant contribution to improving the marital and family situation. The therapist decided that by giving room to Andrew to make up his own mind she would also be giving room to him to earn constructive entitlement as well as to earn the acknowledgment of his wife for having taken some steps toward improving their life on his own.

In her individual session Jennifer talked about her childhood without much prompting from the therapist. She told the therapist that her father had been an alcoholic for much of her childhood. He had never missed a day of work due to his drinking, something he apparently prided himself on, but he was at best semi-aware of her activities and, even more important, of her emotional development. Jennifer's mother had struggled to keep the family together during this period, as well as to keep her husband's alcoholism secret from family and neighbors. As a result, she had no one outside the family in whom to confide her distress over her husband's drinking, and instead turned to Jennifer, her oldest daughter, for comfort and support.

When, as a youngster, Jennifer had tried to talk to her mother about her father's drinking, she was told that this was just something that many men do, and that "your father is not an alcoholic." Even years later, when as a young woman she realized that relationships with men were more difficult for her than they were for many of her friends, and she tried to talk with her mother about some of the difficulties she had while growing up, her mother's reaction was one of disbelief. "Dear, I just don't understand why you always focus on the negative. Perhaps things were not perfect when you were younger, but your father and I always did our very best for you and you never seemed to appreciate it."

Jennifer became depressed and angry after these conversations with her mother. She had also made efforts to talk to her father about her growing up, but said that she "didn't know where to start" with him. The therapist asked if it was possible that she might fear that if she were to confront her father directly that he might "crumple," that he might not have the strength to "handle it"? Jennifer said she really did not know about that but she did know that she could never actually ask him directly about the drinking or about his emotional availability when she was growing up. This statement highlighted how severely Jennifer had been parentified. She had been given responsibility for everyone else's feelings; no matter what it cost her emotionally or developmentally she could not bring herself to give voice to her concerns.

Later in the session Jennifer related an incident that occurred when she was about 10 years old that she felt characterized her relationship with her younger brother James, who was 8½ at the time. She and James had always had a very intense relationship. She said that she loved him and felt protective of him as her younger brother, and as the "baby" of the family, but that as he grew older he began to act in ways that frightened her. He matured so rapidly that by the time he was 8 he was nearly 6 inches taller than she was at 10 and at least 20 pounds heavier. He also apparently had a temper, and was quite impulsive. Jennifer wondered in retrospect if he had had attention deficit hyperactivity disorder.

One Saturday afternoon she and a friend were playing in the backyard when her brother wanted to join them. Although she often would allow James to tag along with her and her friends, she preferred to be alone with her friend on this particular afternoon and told James this. He apparently became quite angry, lunged for her, placing his hands around her neck, forcing her to the ground and frightening her considerably. She recalled that her father had been in the house and that she had yelled for him to come out and help but that he had apparently been drinking and did not leave the house. When her friend's older brother heard her screams he had come from next door and had pulled James away and helped him to calm down. Jennifer said that her brother had never done anything this violent before or since, but he had often acted without thinking and she sometimes was afraid that he might do something violent again.

After listening to this story the therapist said, "I wonder if you are concerned that your little boy may develop some of these difficulties that your brother had." Jennifer said that she felt terrible admitting it, but she did worry about that and she sometimes thought her son was just like her brother. After further discussion she also added that there were times she found herself terribly angry with her son and that she did feel this might in part reflect her lingering anger at her father and her younger brother. Having listened to Jennifer's concerns, the therapist began to think about ways in which she might be able to help Jennifer to learn more about her father's background as a way of understanding his actions when she was young. She believed that if she could help Jennifer to find a way to understand her father better and to accept his failings, the process contextual therapists call *exoneration*, (discussed in chapter 4) then Jennifer would likely be more tolerant of her son's behavior as well.

The cases of Michelle and Mark and their parents emphasize how a therapist may actively consider the experiences, feelings, and wishes of both parents and children, even when their relationships are intensely conflicted. The section on the continuing work with Jennifer and Andrew Pear has highlighted the interplay between work with parents individually and work with them together with their children. The following case addresses a related question, "What place do children have in the therapy of their parents?" Many therapists, including some who would identify themselves as "family therapists," routinely excuse children from therapy, even when, from their parents' perspective, they may be at the core of the family's problems. While there may be a number of compelling reasons to adopt this procedure, I have rarely found it to be necessary. In fact, I often suggest that a couple's children participate in one or more therapy sessions, even if this had not been planned or anticipated by the couple. Including children is clearly required when a couple is in severe conflict that places a child in the middle, whether or not separation is contemplated. Children in such families are often in binds whereby being *loyal* (chapter 4) to their mothers makes them automatically disloyal to their fathers and vice versa. They are also typically trying hard to smooth over conflicts, to dispel sadness—to be the couple's therapist.

In other instances a couple may present a concern about one or more of their children as if in passing. They may refer to a youngster's difficulties in school, to a daughter's difficulty falling asleep, to a son's frequent somatic complaints or fears, or to their highly conflicted relationships with their brothers or sisters. All of these are reasons to offer the possibility of the child or children attending at least one session during which the concern may be informally assessed with future therapy or other services contingent on that assessment.

Judy and Steve were in their early forties and had been married for 20 years when they sought treatment. The therapist began the first session by asking each of them about their concerns. Judy responded that she felt unfulfilled, that she was unsure about continuing in the marriage, and that while she felt her husband was a "good person" and a "good father" he was no longer exciting or romantic. Finally she said that she thought her husband was seriously depressed and needed help but that he denied there was anything wrong, just repeating that if she would stop nagging and be a little more pleasant everything would be fine. Steve at first said that he was there because Judy had asked him to be but that he was unsure that psychology or any form of therapy really had anything to offer them. As the session progressed Steve *did* talk about his stress at work, his unhappiness with his job, and the lack of both personal and financial rewards. He added that he had stopped exercising, had been drinking what he considered to be a lot, had gained a great deal of weight, and was not sleeping well. When the therapist asked how bad the unhappiness got, Steve said, "Pretty bad, but not so bad that I would do anything stupid."

Judy and Steve had four children, three girls aged 7, 10, and 12, and a boy, 15. Although neither Judy nor Steve initially said anything about their children, the therapist made a special point of asking about them. Steve said he thought they were doing "fine," but Judy said that she was concerned about them. Their middle daughter seemed to be having trouble with peers in fifth grade and their son had recently been uncharacteristically irritable and short-tempered. Even after talking about the children and her concerns, however, Judy was surprised, as was Steve, when their therapist suggested that at some point in the future it might be useful for the children to attend a session. They said that they were not sure if that was a good idea; they felt the children should not be present when they discussed their marital problems. After the therapist explained that she was also concerned about the children and how the marital stress was affecting them, and especially after it became clear that Steve's and Judy's privacy would be respected, they were visibly more comfortable with the idea of a session for the whole family.

3

ACKNOWLEDGING
EFFORTS

The central role played by acknowledgment was previewed in the first chapter. Here we examine this important concept and its related techniques in detail. All forms of acknowledgment involve giving a person credit for something they have done or tried to do, or for something that has happened to them. By giving credit to someone we bear witness to events in their lives; by acknowledging his or her past experiences we validate their occurrence and can begin to explore their impact.

A therapist's acknowledgment can help people to move toward more balanced relationships. Acknowledging how a person was unfairly hurt in the past may decrease the intensity with which they cling to that past to justify getting what they want; it may also stimulate people to notice and give credit to each other's efforts to change and to help each other. Directly acknowledging people's efforts to improve their situation may facilitate their ability to give credit to themselves. The most effective focus of acknowledgment will depend on the specifics of the case. A man who carries decades-old resentments for unfair treatment in childhood may need to hear his therapist explicitly talk about that unfairness before he can trust enough to move to other concerns. A woman who is at home with three young children may be suffering for lack of acknowledgment of the difficulties and challenges inherent in her situation. Anyone who has recently suffered the loss of a parent, a spouse, or a child deserves acknowledgment of their pain. But acknowledgment does not stop with empathy; it requires that we validate both the reality of the person's experience and its consequences.

The description of the first sessions with the Pear family included several examples of how acknowledgment can further a therapeutic process. The technique of calling attention to non-obvious efforts to be helpful, as was done with Danny, can be especially useful, not only in families with young children, but with couples as well.

Shirley and Alan had built up mutual resentments over a period of several years. On the one hand they had agreed to seek therapy to try to resolve their chronic conflicts and improve the quality of their marriage. On the other hand, they frequently approached therapy as if it were a courtroom in which each would have an opportunity to prove to the judge that all their difficulties were the other person's fault. Shirley's major complaint was that no matter what she did her husband continued to be angry, overly critical, and unappreciative. She often suggested that he was depressed and needed "help," a bit of advice that he took as both pejorative and condescending. Alan typically countered by pointing out that Shirley sometimes refused to talk things over; that if something was bothering her she would sulk and give him "the silent treatment." After about six weeks of therapy, and at the end of a particularly difficult week at work for both of them, Alan exploded in a tearful rage in the midst of an argument about the household budget, broke some dishes, muttered that perhaps Shirley would be better off without him and not to be surprised if she came home and found him "lying dead on the floor." Shirley was frightened about both the rage and the talk of suicide and after talking with their therapist on the telephone, made arrangements for Alan to see a psychiatrist for medication.

During their next therapy session Shirley commented on the changes she had seen in Alan since beginning the medication.

SHIRLEY: Things have been calmer. He's not so angry and moody all the time since he started on his medication.

THERAPIST: I hope we don't get into the business of saying that all the problems were Alan's fault because he has some kind of mental illness and now that he's doped up everything's fine. [*The therapist is partial to Alan, emphasizing the importance of relationship issues in addition to his individual psychological difficulty.*]

SHIRLEY: No, of course not.

THERAPIST: The medication does seem to be helping though? Do you notice a difference too?

ALAN: She's right. I don't get that out-of-control rage feeling anymore. It's a relief.

THERAPIST: You made it pretty clear that it was not your idea to see a psychiatrist and that Shirley pushed you to go. Are you glad that she did? [*The therapist invites Alan to acknowledge his wife's efforts on his behalf.*]

ALAN: Yeah.

THERAPIST: Would you say she deserves credit for doing that?

ALAN: Sure. I was too upset to think straight myself.

THERAPIST: Do you think that Alan deserves credit for being willing to see the psychiatrist and to take the medication? [*The therapist invites Shirley to acknowledge Alan's efforts.*]

SHIRLEY: I absolutely do. He's always been opposed to drugs and at first I thought he might refuse.

THERAPIST: That's what I was thinking too because some people won't take medication even if it will help them.

Sometimes taking a person's side means helping them put their experiences into words. While anyone can find him- or herself at a loss for words, the problem can be most stressful for youngsters whose capacity for expressive speech is impaired due to neurological or developmental factors. The actual accomplishments of these children and adolescents may lag far behind those of other youngsters; this increases the importance of acknowledging their efforts.

Dale was 12 years old and enrolled in a special school for mildly retarded youngsters. His father and stepmother sought help because Dale, who had always been very pleasant and cooperative, had become very negativistic and oppositional, both at home and at school in the past month. They said he seemed to fly into a rage with no real provocation, he refused to do his homework, and often made a big fuss about going to school at all.

Dale's paternal grandfather had died during the previous year after a long illness. Dale had always enjoyed an especially close relationship with his paternal grandparents, with whom he had lived between the ages of one and three. He had been quite upset when his grandfather died and his father wondered if this could be part of the reason for his current problems. Dale's father had originally been awarded sole custody of Dale because of his mother's severe and chronic drug and alcohol abuse. Dale's mother, whom he had not seen for five years, had just completed a 28-day stay in a rehabilitation facility and had quite suddenly decided that she wished to resume contact with him. Dale's father, unlike many former spouses in similar circumstances, said that while he had some concerns he felt that Dale should see his mother and begin to spend some time with her. A complicating factor was that Dale's only memories of his mother were from a time when she was using drugs and alcohol very heavily and when her behavior was violent and unpredictable. For this reason both father and stepmother raised the possibility that Dale might be experiencing anxiety about this planned reunion.

THERAPIST: It sounds like you're having a rough time, Dale. How are you feeling now?

DALE: Bad.

THERAPIST: How come? What's making you feel bad?

DALE: Because I done bad things.

THERAPIST: What bad things?

DALE: Not going to school. Got mad. Threw a shoe and broke the mirror. Yelled at Mom [stepmother].

THERAPIST: Your father thinks you might be upset about your natural mother wanting to see you.

DALE: Yeah. I don't want to see her. She's mean.

FATHER: That's the way he talks. "She's mean, she drinks."

THERAPIST: Dale, could I ask you about this?

DALE: Okay.

THERAPIST: Do you ever yell at Mom [stepmother] when you're really angry at your mother?

DALE: Yeah. I look at Mom and my mother's face just pops up over her face.

THERAPIST: You mean you're talking to Mom and you start to think about your natural mother and then you get mad?

DALE: Yeah.

THERAPIST: [*Speaking to Dale's father and stepmother*] Does that make sense to you, that he might be sort of overwhelmed by emotions and take it out on the people closest to him, the people he trusts the most? [*Father and stepmother nod in agreement.*] It also seems to me, although I don't know if we are all seeing it the same way, that Dale deserves some credit for being willing to do the hard work and take the risk of telling us what's bothering him. [*The therapist invites Dale's parents to acknowledge his efforts.*]

FATHER: He sure does, especially since it's so hard for him.

Dale's father accepts the therapist's invitation to credit Dale for his efforts and courage. Receiving this kind of acknowledgement would be helpful for anyone; it is particularly valuable for Dale since the alternative to talking about his concerns is to act them out as he has been doing. Following this session the frequency of Dale's disruptive behaviors markedly decreased.

This result is not unique to Dale. Many children who become

disruptive respond extremely well when their parents can acknowledge their positive efforts. In many instances the anger that leads to the child's disturbing behaviors has arisen just because their efforts to be helpful to their parents have gone unrecognized. Some may wonder if Dale's rapid turnaround actually occurred (it did) and if I am claiming that such a rapid and positive response to being acknowledged is the norm when working with families whose children are angry and disruptive (I am not). This case is unusual, primarily because Dale has the benefit of a supportive and very considerate father and stepmother and because his upset occurred in response to a recent and readily identifiable event. The model and methods of contextual therapy can be extremely valuable when working with many families whose children are manifesting their distress by engaging in disruptive behaviors of one sort or another. I do not, however, wish to oversell the approach. When parents have begun to harden their hearts against their children; when scapegoating has begun to be a regular occurrence; and when children have become accustomed to being angry, breaking rules, and getting in trouble of various sorts, the process takes much longer. In the most extreme cases, involving long-standing and severely conduct disordered youngsters for example, the outcome may ultimately be very poor.

EMPHASIZING STRENGTHS, NOT PATHOLOGY

Another group of youngsters who have profound difficulties putting their experiences, thoughts, and feelings into words are those whose difficulties typically lead to the diagnosis of pervasive developmental disorder. This is a diverse group of neurodevelopmental disorders that includes autism, Asperger's syndrome, and other related disorders. All of these children and adolescents suffer from very impaired interpersonal relationships. They appear to lack the capacity to understand another person's perspective, emotional state, or motivations. They lack a "theory of mind" (Frith, 1991). Autistic youngsters have profound limitations in their capacity to use language and in some cases are also intellectually very limited. Those diagnosed with Asperger's disorder, on the other hand, are able to use language well to talk about objects or events but not about their feelings. Some, such as the "Anthropologist on Mars" interviewed by Oliver Sacks (1995) are intellectually gifted, but still lack even the most basic capacity to appreciate the feelings of others or themselves.

The next illustration involves Marty, an autistic boy whose sister has neurological problems that affect her ability to walk normally. Marty's profound limitations in using spoken language to express his thoughts call for a very active technique of being partial to him. This involves empathically placing oneself in the child's position and then asking a question phrased in such a way that the child can respond with his limited language. This sort of true-false or multiple-choice technique may also be quite useful in a modified form when working with anyone who is temporarily unable to put his or her experiences into language.

MOTHER: Marty has been acting up a lot lately. He was doing well there for a while, but in the last month or so he has been out of control most of the time.

THERAPIST: What do you think is going on? [*The therapist postpones taking the "expert" stance, instead trying to create an opportunity for Marty's mother to help him.*]

MOTHER: I don't know. His sister has been having problems, maybe that upsets him.

MARTY: [*Speaking with considerable effort and looking even more agitated than when the session began*] No.

THERAPIST: You've told me how close Marty and his sister have been. Do you think he might be worried about her?

MOTHER: I don't know. Maybe.

THERAPIST: Might I ask him?

MOTHER: Sure.

THERAPIST: Marty, are you worried about your sister?

MARTY: [*Again with considerable effort*] Yes.

This technique obviously involves a fair amount of guesswork on the part of the therapist. It also relies on some degree of confidence that the child will not simply answer yes to every question or respond randomly. In this case, the therapist had enough experience with Marty to know that as limited as his expressive language was, he would answer truthfully. Over time the therapist and Marty's mother had also developed a trustworthy relationship. She appreciated the therapist's efforts to understand her son and to help him express himself. She, like the therapist, was confident that Marty's responses would accurately reflect his feelings and concerns.

Thirteen-year-old Gerri had problems making friends and getting along with other children for as long as her parents could remember. Her teachers had noticed that she often isolated herself from her peers, and that she overreacted to even the gentlest teasing, frequently bursting into tears or hiding her face in her hands. But she was very bright, always earned top grades, and had, up until very recently, never been disruptive or caused any problems in class. Her only real interest was in drawing pictures of zoo animals, something at which she excelled. Her older sister had been shy and somewhat introverted as a child but had bloomed as an adolescent; everyone assumed that Gerri would develop along similar lines.

But when she began to go through puberty things got worse instead of better. She became acutely aware of her inability to form friendships and of the constant rejection she received at school. Gerri was often both angry and depressed about her situation. Her school performance deteriorated markedly and she began to complain about having to go to school. Her teachers began to complain that she would scream and cry "hysterically" for no apparent reason. Her homeroom teacher said that Gerri had once been so distraught at not being recognized when she raised her hand that she had rolled on the floor and said she would rather be dead.

Her parents sought the advice of a psychologist experienced

in working with severely disturbed children. After carefully reviewing Gerri's medical and school records and interviewing both Gerri and her parents, the psychologist concluded that many of Gerri's problems reflected Asperger's syndrome. She made a number of recommendations to Gerri's parents: to look into finding an appropriate specialized school for Gerri, to arrange for her to participate in some group activities so that she might develop at least rudimentary socialization skills, and that she participate in therapy with her parents. Gerri's parents followed all these recommendations; the following excerpt is drawn from a session that occurred about six months into therapy.

THERAPIST: How is school going?

GERRI: The same. Okay I guess.

THERAPIST: And how are you feeling Gerri?

GERRI: I don't know. [*Gerri scrunches up in her chair while she says this.*]

THERAPIST: It seems like that's a hard question for you.

GERRI: Yes.

THERAPIST: [*To Gerri's parents*] Would it be okay if I ask Gerri a little more about this?

MOTHER: Sure, that's why we're here.

THERAPIST: Is that okay with you Gerri?

GERRI: Yes.

THERAPIST: Gerri. I know this is really difficult, but if you could tell your parents and me a little bit more about how you are feeling we might be able to help you more. [*The therapist acknowledges Gerri's distress and emphasizes that her parents and the therapist are working together to help her. As in the previous vignette, the therapist avoids the expert role in favor of giving credit to a child's parents, as well as giving them opportunities to help their child.*]

GERRI: [*Turning away from the therapist, burying her head in her mother's lap. She is clearly very upset, seemingly on the verge of tears; the reason, however, is not at all clear.*] I'm sorry. I'll try to do better.

THERAPIST: [*To Mother*] Do you think that Gerri felt I was being critical of her?

MOTHER: She might have. She overreacts and she is so sensitive to criticism.

THERAPIST: Gerri, Does it seem like the teachers criticize you a lot?

GERRI: Yes.

THERAPIST: More than the other kids?

GERRI: Much more. They never pick on anyone but me. And the kids pick on me all the time too. They hate me.

THERAPIST: Is that why you don't want to go to school?

GERRI: I hate school.

THERAPIST: You do?

GERRI: I try to do the right thing but I can't.

THERAPIST: [*To Mother*] Does it seem that way to you too, that she really tries to do the right thing?

MOTHER: Yes. She does try and then she gets so frustrated and upset. [*Both mother and therapist acknowledge Gerri's efforts rather than focusing on her pathology.*]

CHOOSING SIDES

All the people who are affected by the course of therapy are entitled to equal consideration, but at any given moment one person may be entitled to more consideration than another. There are times when we choose to take one person's side in order to help him state his side. In working with couples this may be the person in the relationship who appears reluctant to state his own side, perhaps out of overconcern for how his spouse or partner might react. As a general rule, the needs of all children are given priority, reflecting their dependency and vulnerability. When working with a family with young children, we may choose to lend our support to a child in order to give voice to his or her side of a situation. This is often absolutely essential when we work with children suffering from significant cognitive impairments, as the next therapy excerpt illustrates. As the excerpt also illustrates, we need not absolutely ignore the other person's feelings and needs, but we may pay relatively less attention to them at that time.

Twelve-year-old Joey suffered from profound neurodevelopmental delays. He had a very limited capacity to express himself verbally; he spoke little and in a highly idiosyncratic manner. His capacity for developing normal interpersonal relationships was equally limited. While he did recognize and respond to his parents, siblings, teachers, and therapist, he had no friends among children of his age. His few interests were very narrow, rigid, and stereotyped. For six months he was totally preoccupied by clocks and time telling; for the next year he was interested only in maps. Joey's nonverbal intelligence had been estimated to be in the average range, and his ability to do mental calculations involving the calendar was impressive. Among his parents' concerns were his "strangeness" and the way he behaved in public. He had been diagnosed as autistic before his fourth birthday.

At first it might seem that engaging a youngster with such severely impaired functioning in therapy might be a fruitless endeavor. In fact, however, many youngsters like Joey can and do benefit from therapy that focuses on acknowledging their efforts and those of their families. Here we see the therapist considering the experiences and feelings of both Joey and his parents, but making an intentionally strong case for the child's needs. Joey was drawing maps of the road to the beach while his parents and the therapist were talking. He did not participate verbally but he was clearly listening.

FATHER: The other day we were walking along the boardwalk at the beach and Joey was acting so strangely that I was really embarrassed. Why does he do these strange things? I'm sure people are staring—they must be thinking we're the world's worst parents or something.

THERAPIST: What was he doing?

The therapist asks about the specific events to clarify what Joey was actually doing; to flesh out the real world context of the troubling behavior. In asking this question the therapist is also pushing Joey's mother and father to be more specific about their concerns; he does not assume that everything Joey does will be odd just because he is autistic; rather he holds Joey's parents accountable for the implications of their statements.

MOTHER: He was, you know, bending over and picking up trash and then carrying it to the trash can. If it was just one piece of trash or one soda bottle, that would be one thing. But he picks up every piece of trash he can find, and he won't stop. It's like he just can't quit. It's very embarrassing.

THERAPIST: From the way you're describing it, it doesn't sound like he's doing anything wrong. He doesn't hurt anybody or take things out of people's hands or anything? [*The therapist explicitly raises Joey's side, speaking for him.*]

MOTHER: No, but he's really weird. I mean anybody could see that he just isn't normal.

THERAPIST: One thing occurs to me just now. Do you think it may make Joey feel badly to hear himself described as weird and not normal?

The therapist again raises Joey's side, this time pointing out the probable consequences for Joey of hearing his parents describe him as weird. This is as clear an example as one could want of being partial to a person by holding her accountable for the impact of her actions on another person, in this instance her son. One of the ways to help people achieve more balanced relationships is by increasing their abilities to be considerate of others, especially those who are most vulnerable. By calling attention to the unintended hurt that she may be causing her son, the therapist is also creating a possibility for Joey's mother to be more sensitive to him in the present and the future, in other words, to be a more caring parent. This will have positive consequences for her in terms of increased self-valuation, as well as for Joey.

MOTHER: Oh, I guess so. I really shouldn't do that but I wanted you to understand what it was like.

THERAPIST: I think I do understand, as much as I can without being there, and I think I understand how it might make you feel self-conscious. [*The therapist, unable to give much credit to Joey's parents for their approach at this moment, is able to acknowledge their embarrassment.*] But I keep coming back to the thought that he really didn't do anything illegal or harmful to anybody. In fact, I suppose he was really doing something positive, trying to clean up the beach and the boardwalk. You know there are groups, civic groups and so forth, who sometimes will go out in a park or out on a beach with trash bags and just spend the day picking up trash to try to clean things up a bit. Do you think that from that perspective Joey actually deserves some credit for trying to help out? [*At this point Joey stops drawing and looks attentively toward the therapist and his mother.*]

MOTHER: I guess so. I never looked at it that way.

The therapist is able to draw Joey's parents' attention away from his pathology, real as it is, to highlight his strengths and to give him credit for doing something helpful to his community.

Of course interventions of this sort cannot reverse whatever underlying neurological damage exists. But that is not the goal. The goal is to catalyze a shift away from a preoccupation with pathology toward an interest in strengths and resources, away from a pattern of blaming a child for his shortcomings and toward acknowledging him for his capabilities and his efforts to give to others.* Clearly, continuing to scapegoat this child for

---

*Readers may wonder about the relevance of case illustrations of therapy with autistic children to conducting individual or couples therapy with relatively high-functioning and well-educated adults. The differences are more apparent than real when one focuses of the balance of give and take in relationships, on the ethics on close relationships. After all, "everyone is much more simply human than otherwise" (Sullivan, 1953, p. 32). The cases of autistic and otherwise developmentally delayed youngsters are offered not as illustrations of the bizarre, but rather to highlight the options for and value of acknowledgment in all relationships.

being abnormal or, alternatively, blaming his parents for failing to understand him, risks eventually blocking their capacities to give to each other: the child, by his actions; the parent, by verbal acknowledgment. It would be antithetical to the core of the contextual approach.

The next vignette further highlights how one may help a child who is limited in many ways by acknowledging the ways he gives to others, and how such acknowledgment can have immediate and dramatic effects on behavior as well. Timothy had been diagnosed as a high-functioning autistic shortly after his third birthday, and had received special educational and psychological services since that time. His parents sought therapy when he was 8 ½ because he had become increasingly uncooperative at home and in school. He was not at all destructive, however, and in fact was often quite sweet and affectionate to his parents. During the first therapy session Timothy hugged his father and then impulsively hugged the therapist and mussed his hair. Forgetting himself for the moment, the balding therapist, meaning to make a small joke at his own expense, said, "Please be careful with my hair, there isn't much left." Timothy's face registered surprise and distress, immediately alerting the therapist to his error. This therapist, normally cautious in talking about himself, especially so early in therapy, saw that he must abandon all such predilections in order to be fair to his young patient.

THERAPIST: I'm sorry Timothy, I meant to make a joke. I meant that I don't have very much hair because I'm bald.

TIMOTHY: But you have hair.

THERAPIST: I do have a little, but people call it being bald anyway.

TIMOTHY: Oh. Can I tell you story?

THERAPIST: Okay.

TIMOTHY: There was once a man with horrible messy bushy hair and he hated it. And one day he was walking down the street and someone threw some scissors at him and they cut all the hair off and the man looked in the mirror and saw that there was no hair on his head and he was happy.

THERAPIST: Timothy, did you tell me that story to help me feel better about being bald?

TIMOTHY: Yes.

THERAPIST: Thank you very much, that was very nice of you; I guess you could tell that I'm sort of sensitive about it.

The importance of recognizing this child's efforts to give something to the therapist cannot be overemphasized. As in the previous case, nothing can reverse the effects of whatever neurological damage may have occurred in the past, but giving credit to him directly, and helping his parents to do the same, can do much to take him out of the role of being a "neurologically impaired autistic child who will always be a burden and cannot do anything for anyone else," a role certain to lead to anger and resentment, on the part of both parents and child. For most, if not all, young children the anger and resentment will manifest itself as uncooperative, disruptive, or aggressive behavior, and of course as noncompliance. Even though this vignette presents a segment of a therapy session as it actually happened, one must guard against reading too much into any single therapeutic exchange. It was notable, however, that Timothy, who had been complaining that the session was going on too long and was generally being difficult, seemed to be much more comfortable in the session after his brief conversation and storytelling.

ACKNOWLEDGING POSITIVE CONTRIBUTIONS, NOT POSITIVELY CONNOTING

If the case of Timothy were to be presented in a workshop or seminar, someone would surely ask whether or not it provides an example of what has come to be known as an example of "positive connotation" or of a "reframe." The answer is that it depends on what one means by a reframe. If one means that the therapist believed that this child was genuinely trying to be kind to the therapist, just as he believed that Joey was trying to contribute to a cleaner environment, and that he pointed this out to the child and the child's parents, who up until then had perhaps been preoccupied about their child's deficits, then it *is* a reframe. If, on the other hand, one uses the term to refer to a statement made by a therapist without regard to whether or not the therapist actually believes the statement, if a reframe is something one says simply in order to effect change in a family system, then this was most certainly *not* a reframe. It was not a reframe of this latter sort because it was a reflection of a truth about the actual (i.e., nonsymbolic) relationship between the therapist and the child. Crediting Joey with his efforts to clean up the environment was not a reframe for the same reason. This does not mean that the therapist was blind to the parents' difficulties and anger or to the child's deficits, that he was ignorant of the evident psychopathology, but that he was able to put those considerations aside to help both the child and their parents recognize strengths and interpersonal resources.

I was so impressed by Timothy's story that I have relayed it to many colleagues and have been very interested in their reactions, some of which may occur to readers as well. Some clinicians have been concerned about the therapist's self-disclosure, feeling that it could have sparked unmanageable anxiety in such a vulnerable child. Others believed that the therapist was parentifying Timothy, forcing this young child to meet his emotional needs. Others — and these were all very experienced clinicians — referred to the thrown scissors, focusing on the aggressive content of the story, and speculating that it symbolized Timothy's anger toward one or both of his parents.

All these comments have a place and all deserve serious consideration. The child was obviously angry, and not just symbolically, and it is always a good idea to be cautious about self-disclosure, especially in a first meeting. Finally, the suggestion that therapists should guard against parentifying their patients, especially such young and vulnerable patients as Timothy has considerable merit. Unfortunately, however, focusing on these issues, valid though they may be, distracts from the story's dramatic illustration of the way that crediting someone's efforts to give can change their experience of themselves and others. Timothy's story is not included here to argue against the need to recognize either pathology or anger when they occur. Rather it is included because shifting to a model of therapy based on highlighting strengths and on adopting a resource orientation, while appealing to many, is extremely difficult to realize. It is hoped that Timothy's story, by dramatizing some of these features, may help.

Some people, even, or perhaps especially, experienced clinicians, have considerable difficulty adopting the sort of resource orientation that forms the core of the contextual approach and of this book. This is not because they do not want to look for strengths in their patients. It is not because they lack the necessary clinical skills. And, it is certainly not because of any wish, conscious or otherwise, to pathologize patients. It is, rather, because so much of clinical training emphasizes the identification, diagnosis, and "treatment" of pathology that one can easily begin to view this as the clinician's core responsibility, relegating the search for strengths to a distant second place.

In each of the two previous cases the therapist was actively involved in taking a child's side by asking leading questions, and voicing opinions about, for example, the positive social contribution of cleaning up a beach. At other times we may be most helpful to a child by *refusing* to respond to a parent's verbal or nonverbal communications. When parents wink at us while their young or impaired child struggles to give voice to his thoughts and feelings, for example, we must resist the urge to do the socially expected thing—to smile or return the wink. We will be helpful to the extent that we are able to reinforce the expectation that everyone's opinions, even those of the youngest or most developmentally impaired, are important and worthy of our attention. If we invite parents or older children to meet with us individually, whether for multiple individual sessions or for ten minutes, it is only fair that we extend the same invitation to younger children as well.

FOCUSING ON ABILITIES, NOT DISABILITIES

The final example in this series illustrates how even well-meaning parents can get stuck in a pattern of focusing on their child's disabilities to the extent that they are unable to see his strengths. John and Betty Brown took their 10-year-old son, Bobby, to the clinic because they were concerned about his self-esteem. His older brothers had excelled scholastically, athletically, and socially. Due to a complication at birth Bobby was mildly retarded, and acutely aware of his limitations.

He was especially upset, as were his parents, about the persistent problems with enuresis. He wet the bed nearly every night and so was embarrassed to have a friend spend the night or to spend the night at a friend's house. The Browns had spared no expense in seeking help for Bobby. They were so sensitive to his embarrassment about his enuresis that they had conferred privately with the therapist before bringing Bobby in for a family session.

The topic of the enuresis came up about midway through this session.

THERAPIST: Bobby, your mom and dad told me there's a problem that you might want some help with.

BOBBY: What?

THERAPIST: Well, they said that sometimes you have a problem waking up in time to get to the bathroom.

BOBBY: Yeah.

[*At this point Bobby's mother and father start to reiterate all the things they have tried including various punishments and rewards, withholding fluids after dinner, and so forth.*]

BOBBY: I saw something during cartoons. It had a buzzer and . . .

FATHER: [*Interrupting as if he had not heard Bobby at all*] We've asked his pediatrician about this and he says everything is fine medically. I read about a specialist in Boston—I think he was at Harvard—maybe we should go there.

THERAPIST: Sure, you could do that, but I was interested in what Bobby was saying. What was that about a buzzer? [*The therapist is of course very familiar with the use of buzzer pads for treating enuresis but wants to highlight Bobby's contributions to the therapy and to finding a resolution of his problem. Mr. and Mrs. Brown's apparent inability to hear Bobby's suggestion is a manifestation of the trap into which they have quite understandably fallen, one of being acutely aware of their son's disabilities but unaware of his abilities.*]

BOBBY: During cartoons. They show things you can buy and they showed a bed pad, it wakes you up so you don't pee in the bed.

THERAPIST: That sounds like a very good idea. [*Turning to Bobby's parents*] What do you think? [*This may strike some as heavy-handed, but in this case the therapist needed to be very direct in order to push Bobby's parents to take his suggestion seriously.*]

Ultimately Mr. And Mrs. Brown did purchase a buzzer pad; Bobby almost immediately stopped wetting the bed.

4

ACKNOWLEDGING EFFORTS OF PEOPLE YOU NEVER MEET

Very often we do not have the opportunity to meet all of the important people in a patient's life. In working with divorced or separated parents and their children we may not meet the children's other parent. In working with adults individually we are unlikely, at least initially, to meet the patient's parents, brothers, or sisters. One member of a couple may seek help for the couple's problem but their spouse or partner may prefer not to be directly involved in therapy. Or a couple may seek therapy and prefer not to bring their children in to therapy. We still take as a central obligation the need to be concerned about and fair to all the people who are going to be affected by what happens in therapy. Spouses, partners, brothers and sisters, children, and parents are certainly included in this group of people.

ADULTS AND THEIR PARENTS

Of these the most common involves individual adults seeking therapy. Very frequently such people harbor a great deal of anger and resentment, much if not all of it justified, toward their parents. They have often been badly parentified in one way or another. Sometimes this has taken the form of parental expectations that could not be met. For others the parentification came in the form of being asked to listen to one parent endlessly complain about the other's irresponsibility, insensitivity, or infidelity. In extreme cases there may have been physical or sexual abuse.

People who have experienced the injustice, pain, and betrayal of trust inherent in these and other forms of parentification struggle to make sense of their early family relationships and, by extension, their current relationships. While it is most often concerns about present relationships that lead people to seek therapy, issues regarding early family relationships are universally in the background.

Loyalty

Contextual therapists assume that if a loyalty connection between generations is not hard-wired in, it is so universally prevalent that the potential for the development of loyalty must be so wired. We speak of people *being* loyal as opposed to *feeling* loyal to emphasize that loyalty involves action, not just emotion. In terms of the four-dimensional framework, loyalty takes its place with concepts like parentification and destructive and constructive entitlement on dimension IV, the one characterized as focusing on fairness in relationships and on interpersonal ethics. Feelings of loyalty, which are of course present when one's actions are loyal, fit better on dimension II (individual psychology) along with other strictly psychological phenomena.

Loyalty is not something that parents need to earn from their offspring. Rather, it is something that each generation is naturally drawn to, something that must be blocked in order to be out of the picture of intergenerational relationships. Examples of what seem to be undeserved loyalty occur in clinical practice every day. Some of the most dramatic examples involve children who continue to be loyal to their parents even after being emotionally or physically abandoned, neglected, or physically abused.

Invisible Loyalty

One frequently meets adults who have endeavored to be as psychologically distant as possible from their parents. But the wish to be as different as possible from one's parents conflicts with the intrinsic desire to be loyal to them. The result may be that one succeeds in being superficially different from one's parents only to find oneself being loyal in a way that is *invisible* to oneself and to others. For evidence one need only consider the many people who have rejected all the surface trappings of their parents only to find that their relationships with other adults, with their spouses, or with their children have replicated those of their parents. How many young people vow never to criticize their children as they were criticized only to find themselves many years later doing the same thing in different ways? How many vow to reject their parents' rigidly held values only to equally rigidly endorse values defined only by their juxtaposition to those parental values?

The conviction that unresolved conflicts with one's parents often lead to conflicts in current relationships is hardly unique to this approach. To the contrary, such an assumption is endorsed in one form or another by a strong majority of therapies as well as by proponents of self-help and recovery programs. Some focus on blaming all of one's problems and limitations on one's parents. Some believe that the route to freedom from repetition of one's parents' errors lies in a complete and vigorous eradication of any hidden resemblances. Some believe that getting away from parents, both physically and relationally—even to the point of cutting off all contact—is the solution. Some focus on making unconscious conflicts conscious. Others advocate forgiveness.

Knowledge and Freedom

The principle of multidirected partiality guides us along a different path. If we believe that we are obligated to consider the impact of what happens in therapy on all the people who will be affected by it, we will include adults' parents in our efforts. It is always a challenge for therapists to find ways to take patients' parents' lives into account while providing supportive and trustworthy therapy for the patient, especially when there is no doubt that those patients have been harmed by their parents. But the result is worth the effort if it facilitates our patients' being free of their old patterns of relating. For the therapist to be able to see a parent's side is helpful and necessary, but by itself insufficient. But if the patient can see their parent in a different light they may be able to find enough of value in their parents' lives to exchange their invisible loyalty for a more visible loyalty. And if they can do this, the compromise of rejecting their parent on the surface but emulating him or her beneath the surface will no longer be necessary.

Contextual therapists refer to the process of gaining a fuller understanding of one's parents' lives, including their hardships and difficulties, as *exoneration*. Although it may bring up images of forgiveness, there are several significant differences between the two concepts. For one thing, forgiveness is something one does because he or she is more enlightened, more generous, or more loving than the person who has harmed him or her. Forgiveness requires neither justification nor understanding of the hurtful acts engaged in by the forgiven person. One forgives another's acts because one is magnanimous, not because the other person has done anything to deserve forgiveness. None of this diminishes the effort required of a person who forgives another. Exoneration, on the other hand, refers to a process of enlightened acceptance of a person in his or her totality; of acceptance, and ultimately acknowledgement of the person's positive efforts, through understanding. It does not require that all of the person's actions be forgiven. Indeed, there are actions that may simply be unforgivable. Despite this, one can still strive to develop a fuller, more three-dimensional, and more objective view of that person.

Alfred Adler, the less famous but highly influential contemporary of Freud who coined the terms *sibling rivalry* and *style of life* and catalyzed clinical and research interest in birth order, wrote about the *perceptual screen* that people develop as the result of childhood distortions and that influences what he called their "style of life." One of the most potent aspects of our perceptual screens involves the ways in which we perceive, experience, remember, think about, and emulate or avoid emulating our parents. Distortions in the ways we experienced our parents when we were young children are unavoidable and a direct result of our own immature cognitive development and restrictions in the information about our parents to which we were privy as children. We can easily carry these misperceptions around forever, greatly affecting our views of ourselves and our most important relationships.

It is no coincidence that a significant number of adults who seek therapy do so largely because of lingering conflicts with their parents and lingering symptoms, such as anxiety and depression, resulting from those early relationships. This is as true of those seeking contextual therapy as it is of any other approach. In practice the contextual approach to such cases overlaps with others. We start off by listening. We are alert to signs of our patient's having been harmed by early events and relationships. And we offer support and validation for that early hurt and pain. At this point, however, we diverge sharply from many approaches, from those that continue to focus on the wrong that has been done to people by their parents, from those that focus on "getting in touch with the anger" toward parents, as well as from those that advocate "forgiveness" as the solution to earlier hurt. We instead rely on the principle of multidirected partiality and on our firm desire to understand and consider each person's life experiences and relational context with the goal of helping the people we work with to do the same for each other.

When adults seek therapy, contextual therapists face a challenge to this principle that is not typically present when working with parents and their young children. That challenge involves finding ways to consider the perspective of parents without having the opportunity to meet them, and while maintaining a focus on the patient's need for understanding, reassurance, and support. The following vignette illustrates only the beginning steps in this process of exoneration. These first steps and questions can be applied almost word for word to many cases. For some patients simply hearing the therapist ask the questions will be enough to lead to dramatic changes in attitude. For others, especially those who have been hurt the most badly and over the longest period of time, the same or similar questions will continue to be a focus of concern for many sessions.

Roy Stone, a 30-year-old musician, decided to seek therapy for his intermittent problems with depression and to try to resolve his highly conflicted feelings about his parents, particularly about his mother. Roy was a middle child; his older brother was a surgeon in New York, his younger sister, a graduate student in anthropology at Yale. His father, Roger, prided himself on being a "self-made man" who, having had to go to work after high school and being unable to attend college himself, placed great value on education and on his children's achievements. His mother, Emily, had devoted herself to raising the children and to the family. Roy grew up feeling that he was the outcast in his family. As he recounted the pain of his childhood, it had always seemed to him that his sister received preferential treatment, as the youngest child from his mother and as "daddy's little girl" from his father, while his older brother was lauded for his scholastic achievements and for being "the genius" of the family. Roy's talents as a musician only seemed important at birthdays and at Christmas when his piano playing provided entertainment at family gatherings. Roy described his father as "distant," his mother as "wanting to control everything."

Roy enjoyed his job as an oboist with the Toronto Symphony and felt good about his accomplishments and talents. He was aware, however, of a smoldering anger that affected his relationships with colleagues, with nonmusician friends, with women he saw socially, and with his extended family. It was these last two categories of relationships that bothered him the most. Although Roy had dated a number of women and had what he described as an active social life, he would have preferred to be in a stable relationship, ideally to be married and to have a family. And yet he had been unable to achieve this goal. He found his relationships with women to have fallen into a pattern characterized by a period of intense infatuation, followed by a protracted period of gradually diminishing interest and increasing fault finding. The personality or physical features that had initially attracted him became those that he found most unbecoming, even repulsive. He was clearly embarrassed to admit this, feeling that he should be above such things, but he said he thought that saying everything was part of therapy.

ROY: I've been thinking a lot about this—why I am so critical of all the women I get involved with [*long pause*] and I think it's basically because of my parents and the way they treated me, especially my mother, but my father too, actually. I remember coming home from school and being excited because I had started on a new piece and all my mother could say was, "That's nice but did you get your social studies test back today?"

The therapist was empathically supportive of Roy's situation and unhappiness. When Roy introduces the issue of his relationship with his parents, however, the therapist is alert to the risks inherent in scapegoating them; the possibility of unwittingly encouraging Roy to be invisibly, rather than visibly loyal; and the danger of being scapegoated for being unfair to them. The therapist was also aware of the potential benefits to Roy of learning more about his parents as people. This is the first step in exoneration.

THERAPIST: How did you react when that happened?

ROY: I don't know. Mostly I just felt terrible. I suppose I grumbled or something. I really don't remember. I just can't believe a mother would do that. It's like she *wanted* me to feel like a failure. There was no way I could please her.

THERAPIST: That's a pretty heavy statement. But perhaps that's what you really believe, that she wanted you to feel like a failure. [*Here the therapist holds Roy accountable for what he has said about his mother. If he really believes that she wanted him to feel like a failure, it is up to him to say so clearly and specifically.*]

ROY: I don't know. Why else would you talk that way to your child? And there was also all this control stuff. She was always on me about my homework. I mean I always got good grades but she acted like if she wasn't on me all the time I wouldn't study or I wouldn't do my homework.

THERAPIST: What about your mother's childhood, her growing up years? What was that like? [*Therapist is partial to Roy's mother.*]

ROY: Actually she never talks about it. I guess it was sort of rough. Her mother died of cancer when she was 11. She sort of took over I guess.

THERAPIST: Took over?

ROY: There were six children. She was the oldest girl, so I guess she sort of raised the younger ones.

THERAPIST: So she was the oldest. How old were the others?

ROY: Actually she wasn't the oldest. My uncle Ray was two years older. She was next, then there were two more boys and the two youngest who were girls.

THERAPIST: So even though she wasn't the oldest, she had the responsibility for the other children.

ROY: Yeah. I guess in those days it was assumed that the girl, you know. I guess it was sexist in a way.

THERAPIST: It does seem that way. And it also must have been a big burden for her; she was only 11 with four little children. How old were the other children? [*The therapist notes the unfairness of Emily's having been given parental responsibilities when she had an older brother of whom little or nothing was expected. In raising these issues the therapist directly acknowledges Emily's sacrifices and invites Roy to acknowledge them as well.*]

ROY: They must have been pretty young. I think my Aunt Harriet, she's the youngest, is about 10 years younger than my mother, so I guess she was about 1.

THERAPIST: Do you see any connection between her childhood and the things she does that bother you? [*The therapist is partial to Roy's mother again, suggesting a possible explanation for her "controlling" stance in family relationships.*]

ROY: What do you mean?

THERAPIST: Well you talked about how she was responsible for the younger children. She was sort of forced by circumstances into being in control of everything when she was young. Maybe that's part of the reason that being perfect and in control was so important to her when you were younger and even now.

ROY: [*After a period of thoughtful silence*] Are you saying that's an excuse for her always being on me?

THERAPIST: Not an excuse. But maybe it's a partial explanation. Do you think she was on you because she's just the sort of person who enjoys controlling other people, or do you think that in her own way she may have felt that was part of being a good mother?

ROY: I guess she thought she was being a good mother. But that doesn't make me like it any more.

THERAPIST: Would you be interested in finding out more about her, more about her childhood? [*This is the essence of the exoneration process; learning enough about one's parents to understand them as individuals with their own histories, their own strengths and weaknesses, their own successes and failures.*]

ROY: I don't know. I mean I would but I'm not sure how to approach it.

THERAPIST: We can talk about this more if you think it would be helpful.

ROY: That sounds like a good idea.

In their next session the therapist and Roy continue to focus on Roy's relationship with his mother.

THERAPIST: Have you had a chance to talk at all with your mother about what it was like for her as a child?

ROY: To tell you the truth I've sort of been avoiding it. I mean I haven't actually been avoiding it. In fact I've thought about it a lot. I actually don't know that much about her growing up and I guess you're right, it probably would help me understand her better. Actually, I'm sort of afraid it might make things worse. She can really be prickly.

THERAPIST: If you think it would help, you could invite her to join us for a session sometime in the future.

ROY: [*Laughing*] I don't know about that.

THERAPIST: It's up to you of course. I'm just offering it as a possibility.

This last interchange illustrates several important aspects of this model. It illustrates one way in which an adult's parent might be involved in therapy. Suggesting that Roy might invite his mother to participate in one or more therapy sessions is one way of being partial to her. The way in which the suggestion is made, as an invitation, and not as a requirement, is consistent with the value placed on sowing seeds and opening doors, on providing people with opportunities to grow, not on telling them what to do. It also illustrates how the therapist seeks to be partial to Roy's mother as well as to him. Illuminating a parent's side is not, however, a magical intervention. Although Roy is able to give his mother credit for trying to do the right thing, he remains angry and resentful.

Several weeks later Roy brought this issue to the surface again.

ROY: A couple of weeks ago you said you wanted to have a session with my mother and me.

THERAPIST: That's up to you. I think I just mentioned that you might want to think about it. If you think it would be helpful I'd be glad to meet with you both.

ROY: Well, do *you* think it would be helpful? [*Although the therapist initially takes a noncommittal stance regarding the possibility of a session with Roy and his mother, he does respond directly to this direct question.*]

THERAPIST: It might be. I think it would be worth trying.

Although the therapist directly voices his belief that a session with Roy and his mother "would be worth trying," he does not push Roy for a decision. Neither does he make statements such as, "We're going to have to do this in order to make progress." On the other hand, the therapist will not let the matter go off and die of its own weight. Like experienced therapists using any approach, he will instead gently bring up the possibility of this conjoint session in future sessions, giving the patient time to gradually digest what is almost certainly a novel and anxiety-provoking idea.

The following excerpts, drawn from a very different case, again illustrate the therapist's concern for people who are not present during the session and who may never participate in therapy (in this case, a child's stepmother) and one way in which a therapist may be more directive while still giving clients room to choose how to respond to each other.

Thomas was 14 and had been having a great deal of difficulty

adjusting to his mother's remarriage and to the presence of his
new 10-year-old stepbrother and stepsister, the twin children of
his mother's new husband. He had begun to get in trouble in
school, and had become increasingly defiant at home as well. At
times he flew into rages that frightened his mother and the
younger children. Although he denied drinking or using drugs,
both his mother and teachers suspected that he had done so.
Thomas visited his father and his stepmother, Julie, every weekend, and while he had gotten into a few squabbles with his
stepmother, there had not been the same sort of uproar that had
occurred at his mother's home. The following excerpt is drawn
from a meeting with Thomas and his parents.

MOTHER: [*Clearly very upset, her voice trembling, and on the
verge of tears*] I know this adjustment is hard for Thomas but
I'm at the end of my rope. I don't know what else I can do. It
doesn't take anything to set him off and sometimes I worry
about what he might do when he is in one of his rages. I mean
someone could really get hurt. He's taller than I am and he
weighs more too. I just don't know what to do.

THERAPIST: [*To Thomas's father*] Is there anything you could
do to help Thomas and his mother?

FATHER: [*After a very long pause*] I don't know. I don't know
what I could do. Do you have any suggestions?

THERAPIST: I don't have any answers either and of course you
would want to discuss any changes with each other and with
your families, but might Thomas spend more time with you
than he has?

FATHER: That's a tough one. I mean of course I would like to
spend more time with him, and Julie has been very supportive
of my relationship with Thomas, but we're dealing with her
mother's illness right now and a lot of things are up in the air.

THERAPIST: It would be helpful to know what some of those
things are. [*Asking him to be more specific amounts to holding him accountable.*]

FATHER: Julie's mother has been in poor health for some time but up until recently she has been able to stay in her own house—with some help of course. Her doctors feel that she needs to be somewhere else soon, either in a nursing home or with us.

THERAPIST: And how does Julie feel about this choice?

FATHER: She's an only child and has always been very close with her mother. We've just started to talk about it but I'm pretty sure that she would like her to stay with us.

THERAPIST: How would that affect you?

FATHER: Well that's the thing. I'm just not sure that we could make the adjustment to having her and caring for her and also having Tom move in with us at the same time.

THERAPIST: Would that be something that we might talk about more, perhaps with Julie?

Compared to some of the more authoritarian styles of making suggestions, this may seem mild almost to the point of inaudibility. By showing interest in and consideration for all family members, including both Thomas's father's and mother's new spouses, however, the therapist has increased the possibility that her suggestion will be taken seriously and acted upon.

THERAPY FOR SEXUAL PROBLEMS

The contextual approach, while not a form of sex therapy per se, can be quite helpful for some sexual difficulties. The following composites illustrate how one may help an individual resolve a sexual difficulty even though his spouse prefers not to participate in therapy.

Jack was 30 years old. He and Shirley had been married for six years and as yet had no children. Jack requested therapy because he had been experiencing premature ejaculation increasingly frequently over the past year and a half. When Jack initially requested help, the therapist as a matter of course suggested that he and his wife consider participating in therapy together, starting with the first meeting. Despite this invitation, Jack said that both he and his wife preferred that he meet individually with the therapist.

During this first interview the therapist raised the possibility that a medical condition might be causing Jack's premature ejaculation. Jack had already thought of that and had seen both his internist and a urologist, both of whom felt that there was no organic cause to the problem. In their second meeting Jack talked about how he had found himself recently avoiding all physical intimacy with his wife because he feared that intimacy would lead to intercourse and that intercourse would lead to premature ejaculation, embarrassment on his part, and disappointment on his wife's part. He went on to explain that they had always had a rich and mutually rewarding sex life, and that he was increasingly anxious and disturbed by his "problem."

As a way of learning about Jack's interpersonal context, the therapist began to ask about his childhood, his parents, and his siblings, recording the responses in the form of a genogram. He learned that Jack came from a closeknit family, that he was one of three brothers, and that his parents were in good health and living in retirement in Florida, where he had grown up. He also learned that he and his brothers often said that they had "salt water in their veins," an allusion to their growing up on the water as well as to their father's and grandfather's naval careers. As children they raced small sailboats, gradually working up to larger and faster boats. Since leaving home they had traditionally chartered a large boat and, with their wives, sailed to Bermuda each September.

Jack had joined his brothers on this adventure annually until the previous year when his wife had objected to spending that much time sailing, an activity she had previously tolerated but never really enjoyed. Jack had deferred to her wishes and had stayed at home instead of sailing. He regretted the decision and was clearly angry at his wife for "making him" do this. Was it possible, the therapist mused aloud, that Jack might have acceded to his wife's request too quickly, without sufficiently stating his side of things, and without giving her an opportunity to hear how important the annual trip was to him? Was it even possible that she may have responded differently if she had been aware of the importance he placed on his annual get-together with his brothers? Did Jack believe that his wife was totally insensitive to his wishes? No, he responded, he did not, but he did feel that she could be exceptionally unyielding about *her* wishes.

Therapy continued in this vein for several more sessions. One day Jack announced that he had told his wife that the trip was very important to him, that he very much would like her to go with him the next year, but that he would go alone if she chose not to accompany him. Two weeks later the therapist asked about the situation with the premature ejaculation. Jack said that he had not had any problems for "a couple of weeks," and that their sex life was back to normal.

Jack's case is perhaps as notable for what the therapist did not do as for what he did do. He did not insist that both Jack and his wife be directly involved in therapy, even though this was clearly a "couples" issue. He did not prescribe sex therapy exercises (e.g., Kaplan, 1974), although he might have done so in another case. Instead, the therapist looked first to the issues of fairness and balance in the marital relationship that may have been manifesting themselves in sexual problems.

I was once consulted by Mr. Lemon, a man in his late fifties who suffered from impotence, a sexual dysfunction that interfered considerably with his ability to have what he considered normal sexual relations with his wife. It was also something that made her extremely angry. He had, at her urging, been to numerous physicians in several specialties, none of whom could find any medical cause for his difficulties. In the course of our meetings it turned out that Mr. Lemon had a dream to take early retirement from his job, something he could afford to do, and to spend his time painting. As a young man he had been an art student, but he had given this up to take a position at an advertising agency where he was the art director and had been quite successful—so successful that financial concerns were for the most part not a factor in a decision to retire early or not. His wife's early years had been difficult financially, leading her to be extremely anxious about such issues. It appeared that no matter how many times Mr. Lemon tried to reassure his wife that she need not worry about money, there was no success. The result was that she became very upset whenever he talked about his retirement ideas.

In therapy we focused on several issues. We spent considerable time (relatively speaking since therapy lasted only 15 sessions or so) focusing on the distinction between feeling badly that his wife was so anxious, not wanting to have her be angry at him, and the issue of what was fair. I was also partial to his wife by talking with him about her background and his level of understanding of her emotional reaction regarding financial security. Finally, I asked Mr. Lemon if he thought that there was any connection between his sexual difficulties and his feeling that he was not receiving support from his wife in achieving his lifelong dream. He agreed that this was so. Over the course of months, he was able to more and more clearly state his side to his wife. At the same time, he found new ways to offer her reassurance regarding their financial stability, such as going over their finances in more detail than he had previously been willing to do, to both continue to reassure her regarding financial issues, and to make concrete plans for his new career as a painter. Their sexual life improved bit by bit until it was back to normal, and perhaps a bit better.

5

SHORT-TERM CONTEXTUAL THERAPY

One of the most commonly held beliefs about this approach is that it requires a great deal of time and unlimited sessions. Many clinicians assume that the model is incompatible with any kind of restrictions on treatment length. This belief is often complicated by a second assumption that contextual therapy is an offshoot of psychoanalytic therapy or is a form of "psychoanalytic family therapy." Neither of these assumptions is accurate. As has been discussed in earlier chapters, psychodynamic concepts, along with concepts contributed by other perspectives on development, personality, psychopathology, and more generally on individual differences in psychological functioning, are valued as aspects of the psychological dimension of life. The central focus and concern of the contextual mode, however, remains the balance of fairness in relationships.

The assumption that contextual therapy must be long-term may be due in part to the prominence given a case involving 170 sessions over a period of three and a half years in the best known contextual therapy text (Boszormenyi-Nagy & Spark, 1973).

As such this assumption is readily understandable. It is also inaccurate.

The literature on short-term contextual therapy is limited, but significant. Boszormenyi-Nagy et al.'s chapter (1991) on contextual therapy in the *Handbook of Family Therapy* (Gurman & Kniskern, 1981) presents a 7-session therapy case; Bernal and his colleagues have done considerable work using short-term contextual therapy in the treatment of drug addiction (e.g., Bernal, Rodríguez, & Diamond, 1990).

There are clearly instances in which long-term therapy may be optimal or even necessary for some people and for some problems. Some patients, such as those with serious chronic medical conditions or families whose children suffer from pervasive developmental disorders, may both require and benefit from continuous and long-term therapy. Similarly, some kinds of persistent interpersonal problems of the sort that are often characterized as "personality disorders" may also respond best to a long-term involvement. And therapists seeking personal therapy as one component of developing an expertise in this approach may prefer that it be long-term.

Even in the rare instances when therapy is free of external limits on treatment length, however, its length depends on the needs of the patients, their interpersonal contexts, and on whether or not continuing involvement in a therapeutic process is indicated. When therapy continues it does so only because the problems continue, not because the model predicts that long-term work is required before any improvement can be seen. Even when unconstrained by managed care or other external forces, an essential feature of therapy involves regular and straightforward dialogue between patient and therapist regarding the continuing need and usefulness of therapy as well as its shifting goals over time.

Contextual therapists, like most of our colleagues, would far prefer to let therapy proceed at its own pace, rapidly reaching a conclusion in some cases, developing more slowly in others, and continuing due to the chronic nature of a problem in still others.

There is, however, no requirement that contextual therapy be a long-term undertaking in order to be helpful. This chapter aims to counterbalance the view that this approach must be long-term and to show how contextual principles may be applied when time and numbers of therapy sessions are sharply constrained.

THE PRINCIPLES OF SHORT-TERM CONTEXTUAL THERAPY

Short-term contextual therapy adheres to all the general principles we have discussed previously. It relies on a shift from a preoccupation with blaming, recriminations, and the identification of pathology to an emphasis on acknowledgment of efforts, on the future as providing opportunities for improvement, and on developing potential interpersonal resources. It does not avoid confronting problems but puts its best efforts into highlighting strengths. Like the currently popular solution-oriented brief therapies (e.g., de Shazer, 1991; Furman & Tapani, 1992), short-term contextual therapy emphasizes options for the future. In our case, however, these options focus not merely on problems and their solutions, but also on the broader goals of improving relationships and enhancing people's capacities for consideration of the needs of others as well as on appreciating and standing up for their own needs. If these principles are followed carefully, a great deal can be accomplished in a limited number of sessions; even a single session can be very helpful.

The goal of short-term contextual therapy is that each and every session catalyze significant change. The therapeutic mindset is one of, "If I have an idea or a suggestion that may be helpful and is unlikely to be harmful, why not talk about it now instead of waiting a month or longer?" In short-term work the review of the focus of therapy becomes more frequent, typically occurring at each session, and perhaps at both the beginning and end of some sessions. We expect therapy to begin to be helpful in the very first session. We frequently evaluate our progress by asking patients, "Are we on the right track? Is this helpful?" A response in the negative is taken as indicating a different approach is needed, or possibly a referral to another practitioner, not as resistance or support for "more of the same."

SINGLE-SESSION THERAPY

Single sessions are rare in most clinicians' office practices, but they are standard as a form of case consultation and in various teaching situations, particularly as a central component of professional workshops. The excerpts that follow come from such a workshop, during which I interviewed a family in the presence of workshop participants. The family included 14-year-old Paul, his mother and father, and Sally, his mother's 4-year-old daughter. Paul's mother and father had been divorced for six years at the time of this consultation. Their son had spent the greater part of the past two years shuttling back and forth between them, with some time spent with other relatives. Also participating in this session was a family therapist from a local agency who would be providing continuing therapy for the family.

FATHER: Well it basically comes down to him being out of control. We just can't control him at all. Well, let's put it this way, when he's within arm's length I can control him, but when he's out of reach there's basically nothing I can do to control his behavior. He's hanging around with a rough crowd, a really rough crowd, and I'm worried about him. We're both [*gesturing toward Paul's mother*] worried about him.

PG: [*To Paul's mother*] And do you feel the same way about your son?

MOTHER: Yes, I worry about him. He's always out and running around. We think he's been drinking and smoking marijuana, and who knows what else.

PG: [*To Father and then to Mother*] I can see that you are very concerned about Paul and his behavior, as parents often are with teenage boys, and it's clear that there are reasons to be concerned. Before we get into that, though, I would like to ask you both a question if I may. Are there also things you can point to that make you think that he cares, that he would like to be helpful?

FATHER: Not lately.

PG: [*To Mother*] What would you say about that?

MOTHER: He just seems to care about his friends, that's all.

I am trying to consider the needs of both parents and their son. It is equally important to recognize the parents' concerns and to ask about Paul's positive contributions to the family, a theme that runs through this consultation session. The first moment of the session represents an effort to shift away from an emphasis on pathology and toward an emphasis on acknowledging people's positive efforts and resources, toward helping both parents acknowledge their son's positive efforts. The emphasis on uncovering resources and facilitating acknowledgment is representative of this way of working with all families, including families who have concerns about the behavior of their children or adolescents. Even though Paul's parents cannot find anything to credit as the session begins, the importance of this issue is such that I must return to it later. The next issue is a typical one for families who have divorced or separated and in which issues of loyalty to parents are likely to be present.

PG: Do you miss your father when you are away from him?

PAUL: Not really

PG: Do you miss your mother when you are with your father and stepmother?

PAUL: No.

PG: I see, so you really don't miss people in your family too much.

PAUL: I miss my little sister, I worry about her.

PG: What do you worry about?

PAUL: Well she's only 4 and it's sort of, you know, a rough area and sometimes my mom is out, you know.

PG: Are you concerned about her when you are not around to make sure she's okay?

PAUL: Yeah.

PG: [*To Paul's parents*] I was thinking about what we were talking about before. Does it seem that Paul is genuinely concerned about his sister, that he cares about her and thinks about her welfare?

MOTHER: Yes he does. He loves his sister.

PG: So he does show a lot of caring for her. What about for the two of you? You said earlier that Paul doesn't like to do chores or help around the house, but does he do anything that shows you that he is also sensitive to you as people, that he cares about you the way he does about his sister?

MOTHER: No, not really.

FATHER: I'm afraid I have to agree with her. I haven't seen that for a long time.

At this point my efforts to facilitate direct acknowledgement of Paul's concern for his parents, and implicit acknowledgment of his parentification, have met with little success. It is clear that I will need to be more actively partial to Paul's parents before I can expect them to see his positive efforts. My first efforts at this are directed at elucidating possible difficulties in their personal histories.

PG: [*To Paul's father*] What was it like when you were a child?

FATHER: I had a lot of responsibility. I was the caretaker.

PG: Were you the oldest?

FATHER: No. My brother was the oldest. I was the third.

PG: But you helped with the other children?

FATHER: From the time I was about 9 or 10 I pretty much took care of the younger ones.

PG: Did you mind it ? Did it bother you?

FATHER: No, not at all. I was sort of a mamma's boy anyway. I stayed inside a lot. Sort of a home boy.

PG: Was there acknowledgement for this? Did people say anything to let you know they appreciated it?

FATHER: Oh yes.

[Ten minutes later in the session.]

FATHER: You know we had a lot of dreams for Paul. Like we always talked about how our boy would go to college and you know, make something of himself. Now I'm worried about that, with all the trouble he's gotten into.

PG: Did you have dreams for yourself too?

FATHER: Paul was part of the dream. We were in love and we wanted a child. We didn't have a pot to piss in but we wanted him. And the other part of my dream was to go to college; after Paul was born that was sort of that.

Later in the demonstration Paul talks about the boys he hangs out with and comments that while they often make wisecracks about each other's families, he would never tolerate them making rude or insulting comments about his mother.

PG: So you always make sure that they respect your mother.

This comment turns out to be pivotal. It represents an acknowledgement of Paul's loyalty to his mother. Beyond that, and more significantly, it also represents acknowledgment of her as a good mother, one deserving his respect. The impact of this is seen in her spontaneous comments following the therapist's next question.

PG: I have the feeling that Paul has a lot of responsibility in the family. Does it seem that way to you, that maybe he even takes on some responsibility for helping you get along?

MOTHER: Paul is the key to our relationship. If it wasn't for him, then we wouldn't even be talking together or be here together.

After Paul's mother is given credit for being a good mother she is able to give him credit for helping to maintain the relationship between herself and his father. This illustrates a common phenomenon; by directly acknowledging one person's positive efforts a therapist may facilitate that person's willingness and ability to acknowledge someone else in her family. There has been a dramatic shift from Paul's mother's original inability to see anything positive in her son to this clear acknowledgment of his crucial role.

GUIDELINES FOR CONDUCTING SHORT-TERM CONTEXTUAL THERAPY

Therapists who would work contextually in a time- or session-limited manner must learn to apply the basic principles we have discussed in an efficient, timely, and yet nonthreatening manner. There should be no doubt that it is a more challenging and riskier task to hold people accountable for the impact of their actions on others when one is working under time constraints. It is also more difficult to find appropriate ways to give credit to people and to help them give credit to each other. The biggest challenge in short-term contextual work is not that one will fail to do enough in the allotted time, but that under the pressure of time one may try to do too much too quickly. Questions regarding what is fair and what is not, what one may be entitled to ask, and what one may be able to give are powerful and potentially very upsetting. The therapist must be able to offer enough support to people so that they can hear and respond to these issues and questions. The following sections offer specific guidelines and techniques for conducting the first and subsequent sessions when treatment is limited to 12 sessions.

Chapters 7, 8, and 9 illustrate how these guidelines and techniques were used in therapy with the S family.

The First Session

The first principle is that one must quickly find ways to be partial to each person who is participating in therapy. This may seem a more modest goal than considering all the people who may be affected by therapy, but it is essential that it be accomplished before the end of the first meeting. This is obviously a more complicated task when one is working with a family group than with an individual; the complexity only makes it more important. Parentification (as discussed under Unwilling Caretaking in chapter 1), especially the parentification of young children, must be acknowledged in the first session. Therapists will find it useful to ask about ways in which people (adults or children) have been trying to be helpful to each other, as has been illustrated in several clinical vignettes. Or they may ask about the impact of early losses, hurtful experiences, or other injustices. Therapists may simply empathically express their personal understanding of something a patient has experienced.

An important corollary of this first principle is not to dwell too much on pathology. As we discussed earlier, it would be foolish (and very possibly negligent) to undertake any kind of therapy without first understanding the problem we wish to address, including the presence of any serious symptoms. On the other hand, making a pathological investigation the centerpiece of our therapy can quickly undermine any hope of change. As in the case illustrations presented earlier in this book, the best plan is to focus quickly on possible areas for acknowledgment. When people persist in their preoccupation with psychopathology and in their quest for diagnosis, as often occurs when parents are concerned about their child's behavior, the therapist may wish to redirect their attention: "I have found that many times we are able to help a child a great deal without ever knowing exactly what caused a difficulty. Other times we may learn more about what caused a problem after the child is doing better. It's a choice of what is more important to do now and what can wait a bit."

Assessing Risk

There are times when one's first priority is to assess the current risk a patient poses to himself or to other people, to establish at least a tentative diagnosis, and to make a decision about whether some form of restrictive setting is necessary. An actively suicidal adolescent or adult may require emergency hospitalization; a highly impulsive and reckless child may need to be in a partial hospitalization or therapeutic school setting; a person who is believed to have ingested an overdose will need to be evaluated and perhaps treated medically. Each of these emergencies must be treated as just that—as an emergency. But this does not mean that we cannot simultaneously assess an adolescent's depression and hopelessness and his parents' capacity to recognize how he has been parentified. It does not mean that we cannot consider whether hospitalization is indicated while we work as hard as possible to help family members acknowledge each other's positive efforts.

Stylistic Differences

There are also several stylistic differences in doing short-term work. In family sessions, the therapist will be much more directly involved in the conversation when doing short-term work. He or she may ask family members questions or share observations instead of waiting for family members to bring these issues up on their own. The therapist is likely to share his or her impressions directly, and to do so earlier in therapy, and earlier in the first session. The therapist is also much more likely to interrupt a disputatious exchange, one focusing on mutual blaming for some past infractions for example, to refocus people on what can be done to improve their relationships.

In short-term work with couples and families, therapists are very active in helping people state their sides of issues. This may involve clarifying miscommunications when they occur. We may restate what one person has said, or ask one person what he or she understood the other person to mean. In short-term work we are also more likely to anticipate issues rather than to wait patiently for them to bubble to the surface on their own. When people are reluctant to speak for themselves, whether they are developmentally delayed children or emotionally constricted adults, we may guess at what they are feeling and thinking. This technique has some similarities to Rogerian active listening but is actually better characterized as anticipatory listening; the therapist anticipates that the patient may be experiencing something he or she has not yet talked about at all.

The therapist will generally initiate a discussion of historical issues at some point during the first session, although this may be postponed until the second or even third session, especially if the first session is by way of a crisis-intervention. Discussion of historical issues may occur in conjunction with efforts to be partial to parents in a family session. A parent who appears to have great difficulty being sensitive to her child's need may be asked, "What was it like when you were a child?" The therapist may also be provided an opening to ask about a patient's parents, as occurs with the S family (chapters 7, 8, and 9) when Mrs. S spontaneously starts to talk about her mother. One difference between the standard short-term procedure and the work with the S family is that the crisis-intervention nature of their first session led to postponing talking about historical issues until the second session. The therapist may also simply state that he or she would like to learn about the family background of the person, or persons in the case of a couple or family.

Contextual therapists always subjugate interest in historical issues to concern for the present and the future. This rule is particularly important when working short-term and is one way in which a focus on present issues and possible future changes is kept.

Sessions 2 through 11

One may safely, and in most cases productively, use the guidelines for the first session as a treatment protocol. The guidelines for later sessions must be blended with clinical judgments about the most critical and salient issues for the particular case. Some general principles may, however, be helpful. In these sessions the therapist continues to deemphasize pathology and to emphasize resources, areas of people's relationships that can be used in positive ways to enhance trust between people, self-esteem, and people's capacities to give to each other. As we have seen in numerous examples, perhaps most dramatically in those of children with autism and other pervasive developmental disorders, everyone can benefit from acknowledgement of their efforts.

A second important general principle for short-term contextual therapy, one that differentiates it from longer-term versions of the approach, is that therapists explicitly evaluate the status of the original presenting problems in each session. This may appear to contradict this book's emphasis on resources and away from pathology, but it is quite possible to observe and, if necessary, ask about, a patient's mood, a child's behavior, or a couple's progress toward resolving their sexual difficulties without devoting an entire session to microscopic scrutiny of the problem. This should generally be done as close to the beginning of the session as possible. This helps to focus the session as well as to provide feedback on the impact of the previous session.

An additional principle of particular importance when working under time constraints is that one may be well-advised to deviate somewhat from the usual reluctance to provide direct suggestions or advice before the patient has had sufficient time to wrestle with a problem and its possible solutions him- or herself. Even when one has the luxury of unlimited time and sessions there is always a tension between the benefits people gain from engaging in a therapeutic process in which they ultimately arrive at their own solutions and the pain they may experience during this process. There is no one rule for resolving this tension; each clinician ultimately arrives at his or her own guidelines. Some of the factors that usually enter into such decisions are the age of the person who is suffering the most, their ability to control their situation, the severity of the problem, and the possible risks of letting too much time pass without change. When time is dear these considerations are joined by those of expediency.

There is no firm consensus on what precise number or arrangement of sessions constitutes short-term therapy. For some clinicians anything less than weekly sessions for two years would be considered short-term; others consider any therapy that extends over 6 sessions to be long-term. In this book short-term therapy is considered any therapy that is explicitly time-and/or session-limited in advance. This may range from a research protocol specifying 8, 10, or 12 sessions to a managed care contract providing for 20 sessions.

Termination

In this model one need not think in terms of "terminations" in the traditional way, as rites of passage signifying that the work of therapy has been done once and for all time. This terminology may fit some therapies well, but it is ill-suited to characterizing this approach. Some patients may feel that therapy fits a one-time need. These people may very well never feel the need to return for further help in the future. Others may benefit significantly from periods of therapy interspersed with long periods of time during which they neither need nor desire any therapeutic contact. Kazdin (1995) has recently written that just this sort of intermittent treatment model may be a particularly good fit for many problems experienced by children and adolescents.

The work with the S family (detailed in chapters 7, 8, and 9) provides an example of how a therapist can be helpful to a family over a period of years by meeting with them for 10 or 11 sessions every other year or even less frequently. The family crisis that led Mr. and Mrs. S to consider psychiatric hospitalization for their son was temporarily resolved in a single session. Even if therapy had been limited to that single session, the family would have benefitted and their son's hospitalization would have been avoided. As we will see in chapter 8, after eleven additional sessions Mr. and Mrs. S were so comfortable with the changes they saw in their family that they felt no need for further therapy. Four months later Mrs. S was seen twice to help her deal with a very conflictual relationship with her mother. Three years after that two-session consultation, Mr. and Mrs. S called again with concerns about their son, now an adolescent, who once again had begun to be disruptive and to refuse to go to school. This most recent period of therapy, in progress as this is being written, is very likely to be completed in ten or fewer sessions. The verbatim excerpts from these sessions with the S family also illustrate that the emphasis on sowing seeds and opening doors is in no way incompatible with a short-term mind-set.

In my experience, reassuring an individual or family that help will be available when needed in the future can do much to facilitate bringing therapy to a close, whether that closing is permanent or temporary. When people feel that they must take care of all their concerns before saying good-bye and that saying good-bye is forever, there is a natural reluctance to bring the work to a close. There may also be a tendency for problems to resurface, sometimes with considerable fervor, just as therapy is about to end. Anticipating these two possibilities by talking from the start about the time-limited nature of therapy *and* the option of returning at some indefinite time in the future for another short course of therapy is always a good idea.

6

CONFLICT, COMPROMISE, AND COMMUNICATION

Some of the cases presented up to this point may make the process of therapy seem all too easy. Family members care about each other. They give the therapist the benefit of the doubt and answer even the most unexpected questions seriously, thoughtfully, and generously. They are ready to give up their scapegoating and blaming with little struggle; they welcome opportunities to acknowledge each other's efforts.

None of these cases is fantastical; and yet things do not always go so smoothly. People are often too angry or too hurt to see someone else's side very readily. To revert to technical language for a moment, they have become too reliant on destructive entitlement to give it up without a struggle. And often the struggle is with the therapist as well as with each other.

The case examples we have examined up to this point have been chosen to highlight, clarify, and emphasize those aspects of contextual therapy that differentiate it most strongly from other therapies. This has meant emphasizing issues related to the balance of giving and receiving in close relationships, especially techniques stemming from the principle of multidirected partiality such as acknowledgment, empathic siding, and holding people accountable for their actions. This is one of the unique features of this model, and one that I believe accounts for the success practitioners of the approach enjoy.

ADDITIONAL SOURCES OF
THERAPEUTIC LEVERAGE

The sources of therapeutic leverage in this model, however, go beyond those that are unique to it. One of those providing the greatest utility is the integration of concepts and techniques associated with other individual and family approaches, as discussed in chapter 1. The following case excerpts show how helping people to deal explicitly with fairness issues and with balancing what one gives to another with what one asks for and receives in return can facilitate the effectiveness of other techniques. This is especially true of techniques designed to enhance marital communication skills. In addition, this case addresses an often-asked question about contextual therapy: When does one diverge from the open-ended question, the sowing-seeds-and-giving-room method, and just tell people what they ought to do to improve their lives?

Barry and Eloise had been married for nine years and had three young children: 6-year-old Barry Jr., 4-year-old Jeremy, and 1½-year-old Kate. Barry and Eloise agreed that their marriage was in terrible shape and that something needed to be done. Not surprisingly, however, they had radically different ideas about what had caused the problems and who should be responsible for changing them. Barry had no doubt that if only Eloise would be more agreeable, less irritable, and less moody everything would be fine. Eloise was equally certain that they would all be a lot happier if Barry could just stop being so rigid, critical, and controlling. In the first several sessions the therapist worked hard to see both spouses' sides, to acknowledge their constructive efforts and to help them acknowledge each other's positive efforts. Each of these steps appeared to have been successful; Barry and Eloise listened attentively and even nodded and mumbled agreeably at appropriate times. Out in the real world, however, they continued to bicker and blame. They had no sexual relationship, they rarely did anything together, and each frequently made thinly veiled threats to separate or divorce. This hostility was also apparent in the therapist's office; Barry was morose and withdrawn, occasionally engaging in nasty attacks on his wife's character; Eloise was alternately silent and bitterly angry.

The question of when to introduce an intergenerational perspective to couples or family therapy is always a tricky one. In individual therapy patients expect that they, their lives, their past, their feelings, and, to some extent, their misperceptions of things will be a focus of therapy. In couples therapy, on the other hand, each person expects the therapist to straighten out the other by pointing out the error of his or her ways. Some patients rapidly become disappointed and angry if this does not occur, and quickly. Therapy can thus easily become a courtroom in which each spouse tries to convince the therapist (i.e., the judge) that he or she is in the right, is always reasonable, patient, and considerate while his or her spouse is self-centered, rigid, and pathologically disturbed. Each person's reliance on their destructive entitlement is so intense that they are locked into a familiar pattern of mutual recriminations. Any therapist who works with couples is all too familiar with this scenario, one which always reminds me of a scene of two mountain sheep who had been butting heads and horns to establish dominance over a territory: Their horns became interlocked; they could not free themselves and both starved to death on the spot.

The therapist wanted to learn more about Barry's and Eloise's early years in order to place their current mutual blaming and anger in perspective and to help them move in a more positive direction. She believed that talking together about their growing up years while giving particular attention to how each may have been hurt, exploited, or parentified during childhood or adolescence would illuminate some of the sources of their current impasse. But important and formative experiences do not end when one reaches voting age; the therapist also wanted to learn about the history of their relationship as a couple. She was particularly interested in the balance of giving and receiving between Barry and Eloise over time; what each had given to the other and what each owed to the other. In the language of contextual therapy this is typically referred to as the ledger of entitlements and indebtedness, a concept that may be applied to both parent-child and adult-adult relationships.

Discussion of historical issues had a mixed result. Eloise quickly acknowledged that her sensitivity to what she saw as Barry's perfectionistic strivings reflected her own childhood experiences and the pain of never measuring up to parental expectations, especially those of her father. Barry initially found it much more difficult to see any such connections between his own earlier experiences and the current marital discord. As therapy progressed, however, and as the therapist was able to be more specific in identifying possible historical trends, Barry was able to identify significant connections, particularly with regard to his tendency to be obtuse about stating his preferences and to become resentful when these preferences and wishes were not anticipated by Eloise.

As the therapist continued to work with this couple she became more and more aware of how difficult it was for her to tell whether or not Barry was listening and beyond that to have any confidence that she knew how he was feeling, even in the most global sense. She would ask a question, offer a suggestion, or make a comment and have no idea if he was interested or angry, whether he felt supported or attacked. As her awareness of this grew, she decided to borrow a technique from the phenomenological tradition and simply identify her own experience. "You know Barry, I have been realizing that I find myself struggling to tell how you feel about the things we have been discussing. Unless I ask, it's just about impossible to tell if you are bored, angry, or agreeing." Following this, Eloise said that she often felt that way too and was often confused about how Barry was feeling about her, their relationship, or whatever they might be discussing.

The therapist was especially interested in helping Barry and Eloise to improve their communication skills since it seemed to her that even when they were actually in agreement about an issue they misunderstood each other and as often as not ended up in an argument. The misunderstanding was so extreme at times that at one point she wondered if one or both people might have a subtle, previously undetected, neurologically based receptive language disorder. After discussing this with a neuropsychologist colleague, however, she discarded this notion since neither Barry nor Eloise had any difficulty in understanding when the subject was neither emotional nor personal. The therapist's initial efforts at helping with these communication problems met with little success. She tried clarifying Barry's and Eloise's statements, asking each what they had heard and what they had understood and asking the other what they had intended. She suggested various standard and modified kinds of communication-enhancing "homework." None of this helped.

And yet it seemed that it would be a major error to drop the concern with communication since it was responsible for so much of this couple's misery. It was only after the communication problems were considered from the perspective of each spouses's ability to both give freely and to ask the other freely that there was progress in overcoming this impasse. The following excerpt illustrates how the therapist interweaves concerns with communication per se with concerns about the balance of giving and receiving in Barry and Eloise's relationship.

ELOISE: I told him that I wanted to visit my parents in Florida in two weeks, just for a weekend. I was going to take Kate with me. They haven't seen her since she was born. Usually he wouldn't say anything, but then I'd hear about it later— how expensive it was, how I had a lot of nerve to take off and leave him with the other two. This time was better, he seemed to take your advice: He actually said he would like something in return. He said he wasn't sure what he wanted, that he would think about it.

BARRY: Well, I think I should be able to ask for something since this other thing was not my idea and so it's not so awful for me to want something back.

THERAPIST: You sound almost apologetic.

BARRY: Well, other times I ask for something and she says no or even gets angry just because I asked. There was this one incident a couple of years ago—

THERAPIST: [*Interrupting*] Let's try to stay on this present situation. What would you like Eloise to do for you or give to you?

BARRY: But the point is, as I was saying, she typically doesn't care what I want, like that time I was talking about.

THERAPIST: Look Barry, I don't mean to be argumentative but it seems to me that it's a whole lot easier for you to complain about the past than it is to ask for something now. Eloise has invited you to ask for something and I've been asking you about it and you just keep complaining. Are you embarrassed to ask her for something?

BARRY: Maybe a little.

THERAPIST: Eloise, does it bother you that Barry might want something in return?

ELOISE: No, that's not a problem, as long as it's reasonable.

THERAPIST: Was it hard for you to ask for things as a child?

BARRY: It was not something that was encouraged, that's for sure.

THERAPIST: Do you believe Eloise when she says it's okay with her?

BARRY: Yeah, I believe her.

THERAPIST: Is there something you want from her?

BARRY: I'm not sure. [*Pause*] Well, actually I'd really like to be able to play tennis once a week after work without feeling guilty about it.

ELOISE: I don't have a problem with that, as long as you tell me ahead so I'm not expecting you.

BARRY: [*Surprised and relieved*] Oh.

[*Later in the session*]

THERAPIST: Well, then I suggest that you start practicing asking for things in a clear and direct way, no hinting around. Because as much as we all would like our spouses to read our minds, most people can't do it and I doubt that anybody can read *your* mind at all.

[*Barry laughs.*]

In earlier sessions Barry and Eloise had discussed the history of their relationship. Eloise had been markedly self-critical regarding times when she had let Barry down or failed to acknowledge his positive efforts on her behalf. Had such discussions not taken place, the therapist would have helped the couple to address issues related to their shared past (the ledger of entitlements and indebtedness) before making the statement that follows.

THERAPIST: One thing to look out for is not getting into the old thing of complaining about what didn't happen years ago. Complaining is not the same as asking. And besides, I think if you can get used to asking directly and clearly for what you want it may help with the anger and resentment. It may also help you to stop saying no to Eloise all the time; I mean, if you can start saying yes to yourself, maybe you can start saying yes to her too.

BARRY: I guess I should learn to stick up for myself better.

A PERFECT PARTNER

The probability of two people being in constant agreement about all matters is not high. Some degree of conflict is ubiquitous in all close relationships. And yet many couples are in conflict because one or both of them believe that disagreements over how to spend money, where to go on a spring weekend, or how to discipline the children are unnatural and avoidable. If this were not bad enough, the difficulty is often compounded by the belief that a loving spouse or significant other should be able to anticipate and respond to one's most important feelings and desires. These are the assumptions of perfect parenting: Someone who really cares will be as responsive to our moods and needs as an attentive parent to an infant. The result, as we have seen, is that both the parentified person and the parentifier feel shortchanged, angry, and full of resentment; they both begin to use their anger to justify their requests and concerns. Their reliance on destructive entitlement increases.

As we have seen repeatedly, multiple paths can lead to the same muddy dungeon, the one characterized by reliance on destructive entitlement. Some people have a great deal of difficulty stating their side; they give in to others much too readily, and become resentful, angry, and often punitive and overly critical in an effort to get even. Their justification for finally staking a claim for themselves is often an angry, "I've been putting everyone else first for so many years that I'm disgusted. I'm thinking of myself from now on."

These people *overgive*, not out of a wish to do so but out of an inability to refuse. Despite having done a great deal for others, having earned a great deal of constructive entitlement, they do not *feel* entitled. The phenomenology of overgiving is of having one's good deeds ripped from one by force. Overgivers feel used by others, underappreciated, and taken advantage of. The ultimate unfairness of their situation is that they lose as well. They are stuck in a wasteland devoid of the gratification that comes from helping another. Neither does it contain the promise of reciprocity: Overgivers do not ask directly for what they need, and since nothing comes of nothing, the self-destructive cycle continues.

Others do not overgive; they refuse to give to others. Phenomenologically they represent the opposite extreme, often believing that to give is to *give in*, and to give in is to risk losing oneself. Responding positively to a request from a spouse or child feels like losing ground. In a tug of war on muddy ground the first side to slip an inch finds itself inexorably dragged to defeat. So it is with those who refuse to give: "If I agree to this, they'll want more and more. It will never stop and I'll have nothing left." It should be no wonder that these people are seen by others as insensitive, narcissistic, and, in the common parlance, "overentitled."

Our goal is not to push people into being selflessly generous, but to help those at the ends of a continuum move toward the middle, toward balance. This means that those who are unable to give of themselves for fear of losing ground will be more able to do this and that those who give too much and without the ability to ask for anything in return will achieve a similar balance. Spontaneous giving is just that: One gives not necessarily selflessly, but freely. This may be out of conviction that if such giving is not always easy it is at least right. When people give spontaneously they reap rewards as rich as those they bestow on others. Giving of this sort, as opposed to overgiving, benefits both giver and receiver. The next case provides another example of how helping one person to be more assertive can bring relationships into greater balance, reducing resentment and bitterness.

COMMUNICATION AND BALANCE

The way in which communication issues are handled within a contextual framework illustrates several aspects of this model. Communication issues are central in many if not all approaches to working with couples; contextual therapy overlaps a great deal in this regard with many others. This is one of the areas in which a contextual therapist is likely to offer some direct instruction and suggestions, since it is often one in which many couples lack basic skills. Contextual therapists also try to incorporate concerns related to each person's psychological makeup and to the balance of give and take in the relationship in any discussion of communication issues.

All this is very familiar to any therapist who works with couples. The contextual emphasis emerges in several ways. One is the strict adherence to the principle of multidirected partiality. As we have seen in other instances this includes holding people responsible and accountable for the consequences of their actions or inaction, as well as working to see and take their sides.

When Jake and Janice have a disagreement Janice typically is able to state her preference once, but then finds herself either backing down or becoming angry, sometimes extremely so but not in a way that communicates the focus of her anger.

THERAPIST: How have things been going?

JAKE: Mixed. I'd say mixed. On Saturday we had what I would call a nice day. It was a beautiful day so we spent a lot of time outside. Anyway I thought it was a nice day until Sunday morning.

THERAPIST: What happened on Sunday?

JAKE: It was nice again. I got up early and fed the kids breakfast so Jan could get a little extra sleep. It's not like I was expecting her to come down and kiss my feet, but I guess I did think she would be pleased, say thank you or something. Anyway when she got up it was like she was a totally different person, and she has been nasty, irritable, grumpy, and angry since then. I had thought we were making progress here and things were finally going better, but—

JANICE: I told you I wasn't being nasty. I just didn't feel well, that's all.

THERAPIST: Could you tell me a little more about Saturday?

JANICE: It was a nice day. I thought maybe we could go to the beach or take the kids to the zoo or something but Jake said we needed to work on the yard, and it was sort of a mess so I said okay. I thought that maybe we could go do something on Sunday though.

THERAPIST: I see. What did you decide to do on Sunday?

JANICE: That's just it. We didn't really decide. We said we would talk about it later. But what happened was it rained in the middle of the afternoon on Saturday so we didn't get everything done that Jake had hoped to so we were going to do more yard work on Sunday.

THERAPIST: You said you didn't get everything done that Jake had hoped. What had *you* hoped to do?

JANICE: To tell you the truth, I really didn't care how much we got done. I was just going along with the program—I really was looking forward to Sunday when we could relax and do something as a family.

THERAPIST: It sounds like you were pretty disappointed when that didn't happen.

JANICE: I guess so.

THERAPIST: Do you think that your not feeling well on Sunday morning might have something to do with that?

JANICE: I guess so.

THERAPIST: From what you've been saying, I think you were angry. Actually I think you are still angry about having to spend another day on the yard when you could have been at the zoo or the beach.

JANICE: You're right I am angry. [*Turning to Jake*] Well how come you never listen to what I want to do? All you care about is the lawn. Why can't you ever relax? It's just do the lawn, paint the trim, clean the gutters. There's more to life.

THERAPIST: You dislike the yard work?

JANICE: That's not it. Actually I can get into it once in a while. It's just that I would like to do other things too.

THERAPIST: Jake, is there anything you would like to say here?

JAKE: Well yeah. I just don't think she's being fair. I never said we couldn't go to the zoo. I just said I thought we ought to clean up the yard first.

THERAPIST: Is there anything to what Janice is saying, that you often put work before fun?

JAKE: I guess so. But it's not because I want to. Besides, I didn't know this beach thing was such a big deal.

JANICE: How could you not know?

JAKE: Well, you only mentioned it once and when I reminded you that we hadn't done the lawn yet you seemed to agree with me.

THERAPIST: You really thought that Janice was agreeing with you.

JAKE: Up until now I did. It's pretty clear that I was wrong.

THERAPIST: Maybe it will help if we go over this one step at a time. Janice, how did you originally bring up the idea of a trip to the beach?

JANICE: It was a beautiful weekend. It was practically the first weekend in a month when it hadn't been raining and we hadn't done much of anything together for a long time so I mentioned that it might be nice to go to the beach for the day. But he wanted to work on the lawn. I mean the lawn will not go away. Why is the lawn so goddamn important anyway?

THERAPIST: Did you say anything after that?

JANICE: No. [*Pause*] He can be so convincing about these things. I mean afterward I can't believe it, but at the time I guess it sort of made sense.

THERAPIST: You decided he was right, that the lawn was more important?

JANICE: No. I just didn't want to argue about it.

THERAPIST: But you didn't really agree with him?

JANICE: No, I didn't. I thought I made it pretty obvious. I mean when he said we should work on the yard again on Sunday I sort of grumbled and said "okay." I thought he would figure it out.

THERAPIST: How would you rate yourself as a listener Jake?

JAKE: You mean like did I know that Janice was unhappy about the yard work?

THERAPIST: Yes.

JAKE: I guess I sort of knew but I didn't pay a lot of attention to it.

THERAPIST: You had pretty much decided how you should spend the weekend and you were not going to be swayed easily from your path.

JAKE: [*Laughing a bit*] That's about right.

THERAPIST: I guess the question is: How much room does that allow for negotiation or compromise? Especially if Janice is not used to more direct confrontation.

At this point the therapist talked with Janice and Jake about their assumptions regarding how disagreements should be handled. She led them through some exercises to clarify communication and to give them the experience of enhanced communication. These exercises were crafted to help Jake to be a more attentive, sensitive, and responsive listener and to help Janice be a more assertive, clear, and direct speaker. In later sessions this couple told the therapist that they continued to have disagreements and differences of opinion, but that these less and less frequently led to angry impasses.

Nowhere is a resource orientation more important than in working with couples. Typically by the time a couple has decided to seek therapy things have gotten pretty bad. It is not at all unusual for the therapist to hear that the couple no longer has a sexual relationship, that they have thought seriously about separation or divorce, and that they argue "constantly." And yet there is typically a reservoir of trust and caring, although the more appropriate image may be that of an aquifer, buried deep beneath the surface but of great potential value if a way can be found to pipe it up. There may be possibilities for us to facilitate this discovery of the aquifer if we can catalyze an interest in recognizing each other's efforts to give or to be caring. When a husband complains that his wife is always annoying him with reminders to take his vitamins, and to eat his broccoli and whole grain bread when he might prefer steak and potatoes, we may ask the husband if he can see that his wife may be motivated by caring, even though he may resent her efforts to control his diet. Similarly, when one person is upset at the other's "constant complaints" we may ask if it is at least of some value that his spouse or partner is able to raise issues, rather than letting them fester as some might do.

LOYALTY, LOYALTY CONFLICTS, AND SPLIT LOYALTY

A rather different form of conflict figures prominently in working with many couples, and is especially salient in working with families with young children. Loyalty has a common sense meaning, one that overlaps but does not coincide precisely with its use in the contextual model. In everyday language we talk about team loyalty, company loyalty, party loyalty, even the loyalty of thieves for each other. The essence of all these loyalties is that they are noncompeting; one may feel highly loyal to the hometown team, to the corporation, and to a political party, without experiencing any conflict. Connections to political parties and sports teams are elective; even in instances when there are competing obligations, these do not carry the power of conflicts in family relationships that are, by definition, nonelective.

But if we turn from thinking about *feeling* loyal and consider what it means to *be* loyal, the circumstances change dramatically. If we add to this shift a focus on family relationships, the possibilities for conflict increase enormously. These are the conflicts we want to be alert to, and of course the conflicts we hope to be able to help people resolve through communication and compromise. Being loyal, as opposed to just feeling loyal, often requires action, sometimes verbal, and sometimes nonverbal. Loyalty conflicts are everywhere in our lives and are unavoidable. How many couples are faced with choosing whose extended family to visit for Thanksgiving or Christmas?

If such decisions are difficult for adults, they are incapacitating for children. And yet children whose parents are separated or divorced face these decisions, or more subtle versions of them, every day. Older children may be invited or even required to provide testimony in court or to express their preferences regarding custody or visitation to a court-appointed psychologist. Younger children may be spared a court appearance but are often subjected to overt influence or covert manipulation by one or both parents. People of all ages may also be put in situations of more subtle loyalty conflicts: They may be pushed to decide whose side to take when their parents are in deep conflict. This last applies equally to 10-year-olds with parents in their thirties and to 30-year-olds with parents in their fifties; The major difference is that 10-year-olds, being dependent and in a process of cognitive and emotional maturation, are much more vulnerable to the impact of such competing loyalties.

The next case involves a situation that could easily have led to loyalty conflicts of the most profound type for the youngster involved. The fact that they did not attests to his mother's capacity to put the child's need for a continuing connection with his father before any anger she may have felt toward her ex-husband. The concept of giving and the importance of being able to give is also highlighted here. In this excerpt mother and child are talking about the possibility of a visit to his father, whom he has not seen in some time.

MOTHER: I hope that Tony doesn't feel that I kept him from his father.
TONY: I don't like him. He used to beat me all the time.
MOTHER: No. No. That's wrong. He only hit you three times in his entire life. And when he did, he sat and cried like a baby.
THERAPIST: Who sat and cried?
MOTHER: His father. He felt very badly about it.

Mother's capacity to credit her ex-husband is striking. In doing so she perhaps provides an opportunity for Tony to preserve some positive feelings about his father, who he has not seen at all for four years, and very little before that.

THERAPIST: Why do you think that Tony says his father hit him all the time?
MOTHER: Because when Tony was very young he used to see his father hit me. I think it's clouded his memory.
THERAPIST: Oh. Is that why you don't like him? Because he hit your mom?
TONY: Yeah.

Tony's mother does not take advantage of his loyalty to her, does not, as she easily could, use it to turn him against his father. In fact, she takes the opposite tack, encouraging him to see his father and defending her ex-husband as a father while she is quite clear-headed in her assessment of him as a husband. As the session from which this excerpt is drawn continued, the therapist quite directly acknowledged this mother's capacity to put her own hurts and anger aside in order to support her son's relationship with his father.

This next vignette illustrates two recurrent themes in contextual work with families who have younger children. It illustrates the devastating effects that split loyalty can have on a developing child, and in this way stands in contrast to the previous example as well as to the single session consultation with Paul's family, which was remarkable for the cooperation between separated parents (see page 92).

Mary was 13 years old when she was brought to the clinic for evaluation. She had admitted to smoking cigarettes and to drinking alcohol. Like Paul, she had been described as "out of control and wild." There had been questions about possible drug use. She talked freely about her 14-year-old boyfriend, and at times seemed to imply that she had also become involved in some way with a man in his early twenties.

Her parents had divorced when she was 6 years old and had

conducted a long, expensive, and bitter legal battle for custody. Despite the continuing bitterness between Mary's parents, the judge ultimately awarded joint custody with joint physical custody. Mary was to spend 3 days each week with her father and 4 days with her mother. Needless to say, the plan had not worked out well. Both Mary's father and mother frequently maneuvered Mary into complaining about the other. Both relied on her to reassure them that she loved them, and that they were good parents. Both parents were also extremely free with criticism of the other parent.

Her father had said that Mary's mother was "mentally ill" and that it was she who needed a "psychiatrist," not Mary. Mary's mother had accused her father of being an active alcoholic and drug addict. Mary's mother had brought her to the clinic following a verbal and physical confrontation during which Mary had screamed and sworn at her, thrown a lamp, and then run out into the street. Mary's mother had called the police who then brought both of them to the clinic.

The therapist met with Mary and her mother every day for a week in hopes of helping avoid another blow up. The therapist also called Mary's father several times each day to try to arrange a meeting; after several days of such telephone calls he agreed to make an appointment to meet alone with the therapist. In the first meeting with Mary's father the therapist found little to acknowledge and was especially vexed with his persistent blaming of Mary's mother. Seeing little point in encouraging this man's diatribe against his ex-wife, the therapist changed his approach. Parallel with the ideas we have discussed earlier, the therapist believed that for a father to be so insensitive to the bind in which he was placing his daughter, so insensitive to the ways in which she had been continually hurt by hearing about her mother's failings again and again, he must have been terribly hurt himself during his own earlier life, from childhood on. To use the terminology and concepts of the contextual approach, the therapist began to see this man's blindness to his daughter's developmental needs as a sign of his relying on destructive entitlement. Relying on past hurts as a source of motivation for the present was making it very difficult, or perhaps impossible, for him to give consideration to his daughter and her needs. In other words, instead of being able to say, "I choose to make myself feel more worthy by doing more for my children than I received myself, by trying to make things better for them than they were for me," he had been thinking, "Nobody ever did anything for me, why should I do anything for them?" The therapist's next step was to begin to identify, and to help Mary's father identify, the ways in which he had been treated unfairly, the ways in which he had been hurt, that made it so difficult for him to be more aware of the ways his actions were affecting his daughter. Here are a few excerpts from this conversation between the therapist and Mary's father.

THERAPIST: What was it like when you were a child?

FATHER: Bad, really bad.

THERAPIST: In what way? [*The therapist is partial to Father by encouraging him to specify the unfairness in his childhood. This is also one way of holding someone accountable for their statements.*]

FATHER: My parents were very strict. My father was an alcoholic and he used to come home in a rage and beat everybody up.

THERAPIST: Everybody?

FATHER: Everybody. Me, my brothers, my mother, everybody.

THERAPIST: That must have been frightening. [*Being partial by empathically taking Father's side.*]

FATHER: It sure as hell was.

THERAPIST: I wonder, were there ever times when you felt you had to protect your mother, to perhaps stand between her and your father?

FATHER: Oh sure. Lots of times my brothers and I would try to grab him to keep him from hitting her, but he was so big and powerful that he would just push us away with one arm.

This is as clear, concrete, and frightening an example of a child being compelled to choose between his parents as one is likely to encounter. The line of battle was active by the time Mary's father reached his ninth birthday. His mother actually did rely on him and the other children to stand between her husband and herself. At this point the therapist felt that he understood how this man could be unaware of the position in which he had placed Mary. He had been so parentified in his early childhood that he could hardly be expected to be aware of how he was parentifying his own child. The therapist also felt that by acknowledging some of the injustice in Mary's father's childhood he had been able to be partial to him. The next step then was to see if Mary's father could extend his awareness to his child. Mary and her father were seen for a joint session the following week during which Mary's father reiterated some of his experiences as a child, especially those related to being in the middle of battling parents.

THERAPIST: Do you think it might sometimes feel like that for Mary too, that she might feel caught between you and her mother the way you were caught between your parents?

FATHER: Maybe.

THERAPIST: Would it be all right with you if I ask Mary about this?

FATHER: Sure, go ahead. That's why we're here.

THERAPIST: Mary, do you ever feel that way, sort of caught between your parents, each one wanting you on their side?

MARY: All the time. Once they were pulling me, my father had one arm and my mother had the other arm and they were pulling me in two directions. It really hurt.

It would be difficult to find a more graphic illustration of the phenomenon of split loyalty than this. From a contextual perspective it is also no surprise that this young girl has been engaging in a variety of potentially very dangerous behaviors.

For there is truly no way she can win as long as she is the trophy over which her parents are struggling and battling. Being loyal to one parent automatically makes her disloyal to the other parent. This is an untenable situation for anyone; it is particularly dangerous for an impulsive adolescent who has already demonstrated her potential for engaging in risky behaviors. As she gets older the situation has the potential to become more and more untenable, and her risk-taking behaviors more and more dangerous, even to the point of suicidal behavior.

PART TWO

≈

DEMONSTRATION OF SHORT-TERM CONTEXTUAL THERAPY

Up to this point we have examined the building blocks of contextual therapy. In the next three chapters we will see how these pieces fit together as a therapeutic process unfolds over twelve family sessions and two follow-up sessions with one family member. In addition to containing many illustrations of such basic contextual techniques as multidirected partiality, giving room, sowing seeds, and others, these sessions also illustrate how the approach can be helpful in a few sessions without requiring a narrow focus on pathology or symptom change.

The following material illustrates how the emphasis on resources, on looking for areas deserving acknowledgment, can catalyze a process of change. In addition, issues such as the integration of historical and present material and the integration of individual sessions with conjoint sessions will be illustrated.

HOW THIS MATERIAL WAS OBTAINED

Unlike earlier illustrative material, this case is not a composite; rather it is based on work with one family. With the exception of the initial evaluation session, each session of this family's therapy was videotaped. The videotapes were reviewed with the goal of selecting segments that would accomplish three objectives: to paint a portrait of the family rich enough in detail to allow readers to know them as real people, to illustrate the techniques that have been presented in this book, and to highlight the change points during the therapeutic process.

In editing the transcribed videotape segments I tried to keep them as true to the original sessions as possible. Nearly all of my statements and questions have been included verbatim, as have the comments of Dennis, the child in the family. Statements made by the adults in the family have been edited to remove any references to incidents or to other family members that might compromise their privacy or that might cause discomfort to Mr. or Mrs. S or Dennis. All changes, however, have been made in a way that preserves both the sense and tone of everything that occurred in therapy. Chapters 7, 8, and 9 were reviewed in manuscript form and approved by the family prior to publication. Readers will note that throughout the transcript excerpts and accompanying comments I refer to the two adult members of this family as "mother" and "father" as well as "Mr. S" and "Mrs. S." While this latter appellation may strike some as out of date or even sexist, it does more accurately reflect the actual discussions than would "Ms. S."

7

EARLY SESSIONS WITH THE S FAMILY

BACKGROUND OF THE CASE

When Mr. and Mrs. S called the clinic, Dennis was 10 years old, and both Mr. and Mrs. S were in great distress about his disruptive behavior. They asked for the earliest possible appointment and said that they thought their child needed to be in a psychiatric hospital because he was "totally out of control." Mrs. S told the intake worker that Dennis refused to listen to her, that he had only been going to school when he felt like it, and that his behavioral difficulties were harming her relationship with her husband who had threatened to leave home if something did not change quickly. The worker asked for my consultation during this session with the goal of avoiding hospitalization if possible.

SESSION 1: FAMILY EVALUATION

Dennis and his parents were seen together for a family evaluation which lasted approximately one hour and had the following goals:

125

- To assess whether Dennis's behavioral outbursts posed an imminent risk to himself or to anyone else, and whether a restrictive treatment setting was required to ensure his safety.

- To form a preliminary diagnostic impression of this youngster and his family with regard to the four contextual dimensions.

- To assess Mr. and Mrs. S's capacities to acknowledge Dennis's positive efforts, as well as to acknowledge any unfairness that had occurred in his life.

- To adhere closely to the principle of multidirected partiality, working hard to be partial to each family member and being ready to take the side of any family member who might need it at a particular moment.

When asked to describe the concerns that had led up to her calling the clinic, Mrs. S said that Dennis was "destroying everything in the home," and that he refused to do as he was told, even refusing to get up in the morning or to bathe or dress himself. His father underscored this, making it clear how frustrated he was that Dennis seemed to want everything done for him, refusing to do anything at all for himself. He then added that Dennis had said that no one loved him, that he wished he were dead, and that he wanted "to join the army and die." Dennis had also recently cut the hands and feet off his favorite action figures, something that concerned his parents greatly. Both Dennis's mother and father expressed concerns that he might hurt himself or someone else, adding that he had already hit both his mother and grandmother.

After inquiring into this last matter it became clear that the hitting, while a clear indicator of distress and a problem area, would better be described as pushing than hitting; it appeared to be the by-product of a temper outburst and not a sign of intentional aggression. It also became clear that Dennis did not truly wish to hurt himself or anyone else; neither did he really want to die. There did not appear to be an imminent risk of harm befalling Dennis or others; admission to a restrictive treatment setting such as a psychiatric hospital was not indicated.

Having assessed potential immediate risks, it was possible to gradually introduce new topics and issues to the discussion. As Dennis's parents talked about their concerns I looked for ways to give them opportunities to begin to shift their focus away from being preoccupied with Dennis's problems toward considering possible resources. I did not, however, want to forget the pain of the adults in the family. "It's very clear that Dennis is doing some things that are very troubling and unacceptable, and we will be working on these, but just now I was also wondering if there is anything that Dennis does that gives you the feeling that he would like to be helpful to you, that he would like things to be better?" Both his mother and father were able to credit Dennis as having a tender side and as being particularly aware of his mother's feelings at times when she might not feel well or was upset about something.

During the earliest phases of this initial interview there were several signs that Dennis was laboring under restrictions imposed by developmental delays of some, as yet unspecified, kind: He was physically awkward; he seemed to have some difficulty following the conversation at certain points; he was slow to respond to questions and statements directed at him by his parents. Observing these signs of possible cognitive limitations contributed to my assessment of Dennis's psychological functioning (dimension II) that had begun by assessing the extent to which he posed a danger to himself or anyone else. These observations, combined with Mr. S's intense anger at Dennis for "refusing to do anything for himself" and statements regarding Dennis's sensitivity to his mother's feelings, led me to be concerned about the degree to which Dennis was being unfairly blamed and simultaneously deprived of acknowledgment for his positive contributions.

Many children whose behaviors are displeasing to adults, including a number of those presented in earlier chapters in this book, are reacting to being parentified as well as to being deprived of acknowledgment for the positive efforts they have made. It is especially important to move quickly to acknowledge how these children are trying to be helpful; such an intervention is designed to encourage similar acknowledgment by other family members and to keep options for giving open for the child. In this first meeting with the S family I asked, "Do you think that Dennis might like to do more, if he knew what to do?" Mr. and Mrs. S reluctantly and quite tentatively said that they had never thought about it that way but that it might be so. Although it was quite possible, even likely, that their lukewarm but positive response reflected their respect for a professional's opinion more than any real change in their attitude, I regarded their willingness to consider my suggestion as a positive sign. I then asked Dennis, "If you knew what to do, and you knew how to do it, would you want to do more for yourself? Do you think you might feel better if you got yourself up in the morning?" phrasing the questions in this way because of my impression of Dennis as a youngster who might have some cognitive limitations.

Dennis said "yes," and his one word answer, delivered in a labored manner, further reinforced my impression that he might, at the very least, have a significant difficulty with expressive language. Feeling empathic with this little boy who seemed to be struggling to make himself understood, I wanted to help Dennis's parents see this and give him credit for trying: "Do you think that Dennis might have trouble expressing himself and that some of his temper tantrums might come from being frustrated with his ability to find the right words to use?" Dennis's mother thought this might be the case. His father strongly and angrily disagreed, "He can be perfectly clear when he wants to. He doesn't seem to have any trouble speaking up when he wants something from us." I then wondered aloud, "Perhaps when he is calm he can express himself well, but when he is upset it becomes much more difficult for him." Dennis's father, still angry, said that this might be so but repeated that Dennis could express himself perfectly well sometimes.

SESSION 2: ONE WEEK LATER

The first session appeared to be successful in resolving the S family's acute crisis. The overall goals for the following sessions are:

- To adhere strictly to a resource orientation, continuing to emphasize all family members' efforts to be helpful and to give to each other
- To continue to be alert for opportunities to be actively partial to all three family members, but especially to Dennis, who is clearly in the greatest need of my help in surfacing his concerns
- To help Mr. and Mrs. S come to grips with the reality of their son's limitations. Some grieving over this will be inevitable but it must come on their terms.

Session 2 also has several specific goals:

- To determine the impact of the first session, particularly with regard to my efforts to help Mr. and Mrs. S acknowledge both Dennis's difficulties and his efforts to give something of value to them.
- To begin to learn about Mr. and Mrs. S's personal and family histories, and their own sources of destructive entitlement.

Mr. S begins the session by relating an incident that had occurred while they were shopping. Following this I try to help Dennis raise his side, "to tell his side of the story." Dennis's problems with expressing himself are dramatic.

FATHER: Exactly one week ago, after our first session together, we had a major grand mal temper tantrum in the middle of a department store. He had gotten a $100 gift certificate for Christmas, and it was specified to be used for clothes. So, we took him out and used up $75.00 of it on clothes. And the incident was over a pair of tennis shoes. No big deal. I wanted him to try on a pair of sneakers so we could get an idea of the size. A child's feet grow. "Here. Try these on so we can get an idea of the size." He threw a major temper tantrum because he was under the impression that we were going to get that particular pair of shoes. I tried my damndest to explain to him in a reasonable manner, "No, we're not getting these shoes. I just want to check the size, then we'll walk around and find one you like." He could even pick it out. No big deal, we had plenty of money. It ended up with him laying on the ground, kicking and screaming at the top of his lungs in the middle of the store, and finally I just had enough. I grabbed ahold of his foot, put the tennis shoe on there to get an idea of the size. Everyone's upset; yelling and screaming, sweating like pigs, all over nothing. And I tried to explain to him, if he'd sit down for a minute and a half it would have all been over.

PG: Lying on your back kicking and screaming? What is your side of the story Dennis? When something like this happens, in my experience, everyone has their own story to tell. And I like to hear everybody's story. And I'd like to hear your story about what happened in the store. It might be the same as Dad's or it might be different.

This is a clear-cut example of how multidirected partiality does not mean being equally partial to everybody, and how it differs from both impartiality and therapeutic neutrality. The first session made it clear that Dennis has great difficulty expressing himself; to make his situation worse he has just been put on the spot and blamed. I take his side to help him voice his concerns.

DENNIS: I asked for a toy. Dad said no.

It begins to appear that Dennis's developmental difficulties go well beyond those associated with expressive language and include significant comprehension difficulties as well.

MOTHER: Talk up.
DENNIS: I asked for toys. No.
PG: Is that all?
DENNIS: Gift certificate not for toys.
PG: Not for toys. You wanted a toy, I understand that part, and then your father said no because the gift was for clothes, I understand that part, so far we're okay. Then what happened?

I continue to focus on helping Dennis to express his thoughts.

MOTHER: What happened Dennis? What happened? After knowing that you couldn't have the toys. When we told you that you wouldn't get the toys remember? Then what happened? What did you do? Dennis?
DENNIS: I had a fit.

I continue to focus on being partial to Dennis and on helping him to surface his side. More specifically, I try to highlight the disability under which Dennis is living, particularly his difficulty with expressing himself verbally. These interventions illustrate several aspects of multidirected partiality and further illustrate how extending one's partiality in multiple directions does not mean that we must be partial to everyone at once. I take Dennis's side because as a child, particularly a child who appears to be burdened with a significant disability, he is in the greatest need of my support and partiality. Since his parents have asked for help for their child, any efforts I make on his behalf will also ultimately benefit them; I am able to be partial to Dennis without being against his parents. Mr. and Mrs. S appear to expect and accept this; they are receptive to my being partial to their son. In other families a therapist may need to be more explicitly partial to parents before they can tolerate his or her siding with their child.

PG: You had a fit, okay. Now here is a question that I will ask Dennis, but I think it is for everybody: Is a fit a way of saying something, not the best way, not a good way, but a way of saying "I'm angry, I'm upset"? Is it difficult for you, Dennis, to put thoughts into words if you are upset, or can you do that?

This is another facet of being partial to Dennis; this time involving acknowledging both his efforts to communicate and his frustration over the unfairness of having to struggle to put his experiences into words. My comment that a fit is not a particularly good way of expressing emotions represents an attempt to be partial to Mr. S, who has little tolerance for his son's outbursts.

DENNIS: No, can't do that.
PG: You can't do that. I think we talked about this very briefly last week. [*To Father*] Is that your impression, that there are times when it is difficult?
FATHER: For him to express when he's upset?
PG: I thought I remembered your saying last week that sometimes he is very effective and at other times he is not so successful at saying what's on his mind.
FATHER: He gets excited. He's going through speech (therapy), so when he does get excited he gets a little tongue-tied. You have to slow him down a little bit so he can express his ideas.

Mr. S recognizes that Dennis *does* have problems expressing himself. While he may not have recognized or accepted the depth of Dennis's problems or their immediate or long-term implications, his acknowledgment of Dennis's difficulties is still a very good prognostic sign.

MOTHER: Dennis, now when it comes to thinking, you hand him a problem—"think it out." He has a problem. It's a little hard for him that way, to comprehend. But show him something once; he'll watch you and then he'll show you how to do it.

Mother's statement dramatically illustrates both her understanding of Dennis's limitations and her ability to acknowledge his strengths. It highlights her ability to rely on constructive entitlement despite having accrued considerable destructive entitlement, both from the burden of having a disabled child and from other sources that become clearer as we proceed. Even though she has been badly hurt in life she is able to recognize and acknowledge her son as a unique whole person.

PG: Then he can do it.

MOTHER: Dennis has been doing well in school. He got a B on his report card last time.

FATHER: He got a B. Last year he brought home straight Cs. No biggie, I asked him one question, "Are you doing your best?" He said, "Yeah, yeah, I'm doing my best; I'm trying." That's all you can ask of anybody, just try to do your best. Boy brought home straight Cs. My feeling was, "That's outstanding; let's go party." He brought home a B on the last report card and he walked right past my wife, right past her. He showed it to me and said, "Look, buddy, look what I got."

Despite his frustration and anger Dennis's father, like his mother, is readily able to acknowledge Dennis's positive contributions, both his school accomplishments and his wish to share them with his family, and more particularly with him. There is nothing in Mr. S's manner to suggest that he wishes to discount his wife's importance or her role as a mother by his remarks; rather he appears to be expressing appreciation of Dennis's accomplishments and pleasure that Dennis wants to share these accomplishments with him.

PG: So that relationship between the two of you is special in some ways. He also—I guess I'm really asking you—does it seem to you that in a way he's trying to give this to you, saying, "I did this for me, but I did it for you too"?

This may be gilding the lily in as much as Mr. S has already acknowledged Dennis's giving; my intent, however, is to highlight this giving, to acknowledge the intimacy between father and son in order to facilitate further acknowledgement by Mr. S of his son's efforts and accomplishments.

FATHER: He did it for himself because he knows we both want him to try his best, but he also does it for either one or the other so that particular one will be a little extra proud of him.

It is worth noting that after he is acknowledged Mr. S then passes some of this acknowledgment along to his wife. The next exchange further illustrates Dennis's difficulties with verbal comprehension and expression while also providing an indication of the frustration that might easily escalate to more overt conflict at home. Dennis's mother would like me to appreciate Dennis's accomplishments. In the ensuing exchange Dennis's comprehension difficulties lead to frustration on both their parts. My response represents an effort to do two things at once: to model a different way of talking to Dennis, and to once again be partial to him, to take his side at a difficult point in the session.

MOTHER: Dennis, tell the doctor what you work with in school. What Sally and Gene have at their house.
DENNIS: Cats.

MOTHER: No, no, no. What do they have? What does Sally have up in that one bedroom that you like? It looks like a typewriter.

DENNIS: Calculator?

MOTHER: No.

DENNIS: Desk.

MOTHER: [*Becoming considerably more insistent and some-what exasperated as the exchange continues*] No. You've been working with it for almost three years now.

DENNIS: What?

MOTHER: It has a TV screen on it, Dennis?

DENNIS: [*Baffled*] TV?

MOTHER: No. Whenever we go in Sears, and you go upstairs to the electronic department, what do you go and play with?

DENNIS: In the computers?

MOTHER: You have computers in school right? Tell the doctor how you have been working with them. Tell him about your school day, Dennis, how things go.

PG: You have been using a computer in school, you enjoy that? So you like things better that you can do with your hands than talking or reading. That is hard [*illustrating by making typing motions*].

DENNIS: I hate to print everything — it's hard.

PG: It's very hard.

There are times that being partial means acknowledging the burden a person carries or, as in this instance, the difficulties under which a person labors, those disabilities that make ordinary accomplishments extraordinarily challenging. I make a special effort to acknowledge these here, as I do whenever I work with a learning disabled or developmentally delayed child; my hope is that my acknowledgment will foster future acknowledgement by family members and that it will help keep the child's options for giving open. A few minutes later, Mother begins to talk about behavioral problems of the sort that led to the original referral.

MOTHER: We have been having some problems with Dennis refusing to get up and get ready for school in the morning, haven't we?

FATHER: Every morning.

MOTHER: But sometimes he can be very good. Yesterday morning he got right up and dressed himself. He's been dressing himself. He's been taking his shower at night. It's these fits and that he won't listen. A lot of parents can say to their kids, "Look, this is it, this is the rule," and the kids go along. Not Dennis. You can sit him down and look him in the eye and say, "No way, forget it, you are not doing whatever," and he'll just look back at you as if to say, "Oh yeah? Just watch me." I don't know how he got to be this way. I know part of it comes down to my mom and how she molded him.

Two issues emerge at this point. One is Mrs. S's capacity to see positives even in the face of considerable frustration with Dennis. Some might see this as her "inability to maintain firm expectations and consequences." While there may be some truth to this, as she freely acknowledges a bit later, from a contextual perspective her ability to see Dennis's positive efforts is more important than any temporary difficulty enforcing discipline. The second issue is that Mrs. S spontaneously talks about her difficulties with her mother, providing an opportunity for me to express my interest in her mother and in her relationship with her mother.

PG: I'm glad you mentioned your mother, because one of the things that I've found over the years to be very helpful in working with families is to learn about the families that the parents grew up in. And I would like to know at least a little about your family. One thing I also want to say, and I say this to everybody, is that when I ask about the parents' families I never know what may be there. And I never know if they want to talk about it with their child here or not. So when I ask that question I always tell parents, "If you would rather talk about this or part of it in a session without your child present that's okay, just tell me." But if there are some aspects of them you can talk about now, that would be good.

This is a standard introduction to asking for information about family history. The goal is to give room to people to talk about those aspects of their family relationships and history that they are prepared to discuss without making this a requirement or obligation. A therapist's expression of interest in people's families typically sparks their own interest: Adults generally enjoy talking about their childhood experiences and family relationships; children are always fascinated to hear about their parents as children. When inviting adults to talk about their families I always include a provision for them to talk with me privately about any issues that they prefer to discuss without their children present; I do not regard this as perpetuating family secrets but as respecting people's rights to some privacy.

The information below has been both disguised and truncated to conserve space and to eliminate identifying information. In the actual session Mother provided detailed information about her parents' backgrounds, as well as historical and current information about her siblings and their families.

MOTHER: I'm the youngest of seven.

PG: You're the youngest. Could you tell me your brothers' and sisters' names starting with the oldest?

MOTHER: Jim is the oldest, then there's Millie, Stevie, Joanne, Chuck, Judy, and then me.

PG: And your parents?

MOTHER: My parents were married for over 30 years. My mother had a nervous breakdown when I was 8 years old. She recovered from it but she was never quite the same. I love my mom. I am very close to her. [*Beginning to cry*] It's bothering me because we aren't talking.

Two major sources of injustice in Dennis's mother's life arise from her very difficult relationship with her mother as well as the significant health problems that she goes on to describe. One is impressed by Mrs. S's ability to focus on how she can be helpful to others despite her own very difficult history. Despite having accrued a great deal of destructive entitlement she is able to rely on constructive entitlement in her close relationships. This capacity to try to be helpful to others in the face of personal suffering and loss is usually only seen in those who have had the benefit of solid, reliable, caring and concern from an adult during early childhood. In Mrs. S's case her mother may have been a much more loving and reliable parent prior to her breakdown; another possibility is that her father was the source of this considerate parenting.

MOTHER: My father died five years ago. I miss him a lot. You know, he had a lot of health problems and I have some of the same problems. My father died of heart disease and I have very high blood pressure and other circulatory problems. Some days my legs are so painful that it's hard even to walk up the steps. Our family doctor even told my mom, "You're in better health than your youngest daughter." And then he looked at me and he shook his head and he said, "You're so young and you've got so much wrong with you." I have a cousin who has a lot of ailments, a very bad heart and other problems. She's got so many things wrong with her. It's a miracle that she's still alive.

One consideration is that identification with her father may even extend into the realm of invisible loyalty regarding health problems. This is not to say that being invisibly loyal causes Mrs. S's health problems in some magical way, but that her comments regarding the similarity of her problems to those of her father may reflect invisible loyalty. These pronouncements by her physician regarding poor health, with the implication of poor long-term outlook, might have provided a justification for many people to be insensitive, uncaring, and self-preoccupied. Dennis's mother is clearly concerned about her health, but it does not usually stop her from giving to others. At times, however, these concerns temporarily dampen her sensitivity.

At this point Mother looks over at Dennis, and apparently notices for the first time that Dennis has been looking intently at her and talking quietly. It appears that he is reacting to her statements about her poor health and that his comments, although quiet and unintelligible, reflect this concern.

MOTHER: [*Annoyed*] Why are you acting like this, Dennis?
PG: Do you think this is upsetting to Dennis?

Mother appears to be angry at Dennis because of his behavior while she is talking about her medical problems. I take Dennis's side by suggesting that he may be reacting to what she has been saying.

MOTHER: What?
PG: To hear about this [*referring to mother's medical problems*].
MOTHER: No. Not really. If I didn't talk about it here, he would hear it from my mother. Sometimes I think she tells him upsetting things because she's angry with me.

In contrast to earlier sections that illustrated an ability to adopt a resource orientation despite having suffered greatly in her own life, Mother's response here shows how her earlier very difficult experiences with her mother color her perceptions and decrease her ability to see that Dennis may have concerns about her health or that he may sense her distress at the moment. Mrs. S's remarks about her mother also illustrate the degree of mistrust between them; this is what leads to the split loyalty that I believe Dennis experiences. One might have confronted her on either the split loyalty or her insensitivity to Dennis; my feeling is that interest and support are more indicated at this point than being held accountable.

MOTHER: My dad and I were really close. He would come visit me or I would visit him. If he needed something I'd give it; I would give to both parents because I cared about them. I saw how they struggled when we were younger, you know, with seven children and not much money. And it was rough.

It becomes clear not only that Mother has given to both parents but also that she also feels good about having given to them both. Her capacity to give to her son, as well as her capacity to continue to care about her mother despite a very rocky relationship further illustrates her freedom to give to others. Despite a difficult life as a child and as an adult, she relies strongly on constructive entitlement in relating to others. Where some people might long ago have adopted an attitude of callousness toward the suffering of others, she continues to care and to look for opportunities to give. Mrs. S clearly feels anger and some resentment toward her mother: She is also able to acknowledge her parents' difficulties, a crucial step toward exoneration, and one she has taken spontaneously. Exoneration involves a dialectical process, one that includes anger and resentment as well as striving for understanding. In fact it is often the anger and resentment that motivate one to search for understanding of one's parents' actions and motivations: "How could they have done that? How could they have loved me and yet been so unfeeling, so harsh, so punitive?"

MOTHER: I don't want to be the way with Dennis the way my mom was with me. My mother was very strict with me and with all us kids.
FATHER: Well, she wasn't strict and demanding with all the kids. There were favorites.

Mr. S demonstrates his caring for his wife, his sympathy for her struggles with her mother, and his anger at what he regards as the unfair treatment she received in childhood.

MOTHER: Um.
PG: You don't want to be with Dennis how your mom was with you.
MOTHER: One time, this was when I was a woman. I was—
DENNIS: Twelve?

Although at this point the discussion does not directly involve Dennis he listens carefully, as most children do during family sessions.

MOTHER: No. I was—
DENNIS: Thirteen?
MOTHER: Eighteen years old. I was working and all. I had stayed out all night. And she was waiting for me when I came in. She literally beat the shit out of me. I was beaten so badly that I had to go to the hospital. I was bruised from my chest on down to here. My father and she were divorced. My father hated it when she hit me. My dad only hit me twice in my life and that was with a belt on the rear end. But never like my mother. And I don't want to do that to Dennis.

This is only one instance of the hurt Dennis's mother has experienced at her own mother's hands. It would not be surprising if as a result she was harsh or worse with her son. And yet the result has been quite the opposite.

PG: Could I ask you a question?
MOTHER: Sure.
PG: Not that I expect the whole answer now. It's just something to think about. Does it ever happen that because you so much don't want to be so hard on Dennis, that it's difficult to discipline him? Do you find yourself going the other way?

This is an example of using a leading question to catalyze a process of thinking about the possible connection between her concern that she not replicate her own mother's harsh parental style and her reluctance to set limits with Dennis.

FATHER: Going too far the other way?
PG: In your own judgment, not anybody else's judgment.

I want to avoid the expert stance, the stance of telling Mrs. S how she should be as a parent; instead I try to solicit her own opinion.

MOTHER: Yeah it's hard.
PG: Is there more to that, that we should talk about in the future?

Here I am opening a door and then asking permission to return to the subject.

MOTHER: Yeah, sure.

SESSION 3: ONE WEEK LATER

In addition to the overall therapy goals detailed earlier, the specific goal for this session is to follow up on the question about the relationship between Dennis's mother's harsh childhood and her tendency to baby him. I do not want to blame her, but rather, in keeping with the contextual emphasis on strengths, to help her to find ways to be a giving mother while facilitating her son's development and increasing autonomy. I also want to help Mrs. S engage in a process of exoneration of her mother when she is ready to do so.

PG: How have things been at home?
FATHER: Um, better than they have been in the past. Still got a lot of improving to do. I finally think that he's starting to get

the idea that his mother is not there to be at his beck and call. There have been a few incidents. Compared to what they had been, a few minor incidents. What I'm trying to do and what I'm trying to get my wife to do is show consistency in whatever we do at home. So finally the idea will sink in that we run the home. Not him. The discipline has also been a little better on our part and that has helped.

Father has on his own basically instituted the kind of practices advocated in many parent-training approaches to the "management" of children's behaviors. He also takes responsibility for his role, and that of his wife, in continuing or improving the situation. With regard to the often asked question about long-term versus short-term treatment, it may be interesting to note the degree of change that has occurred after only two sessions, especially the change in Father's attitude. It is unclear at this point whether Mr. S's statement "what I'm trying to get my wife to do" represents support, criticism, or both. Rather than challenge Mr. S at this very early stage of therapy I choose to make a mental note of the issue and look for an opportunity to pursue it later.

PG: [*To Dennis*] We talked some about being able to do things for yourself. Remember we talked about that?
DENNIS: Mmm hmm.
PG: Remember when we first met, and you said that you liked that, to do more things for yourself? [*Dennis nods in agreement*] We talked about that last time. I think we were talking about getting up in the morning.
FATHER: Pardon?
PG: [*To Dennis and Father*] I think we talked about getting up in the morning for school?
FATHER: Mmm hmm
MOTHER: Still having a slight problem with that.
FATHER: Well, yeah, sure, we're having a problem with that,

but it's what he's doing—he's dressed himself, he's washed himself [*smiling and chuckling*] like any 10-year-old boy.

Father comes to Dennis's defense, being relaxed enough to show a sense of humor. The contrast between the way in which he characterized Dennis's behavior in the first meeting, as being totally out of control and having temper tantrums, and his statement here, that he is "like any 10-year-old boy," is striking. Although there will be further difficulties, there has already been a shift toward positives and looking for areas deserving of acknowledgment.

FATHER: It's not so much what Dennis is doing for himself— it's the less amount that Martha has had to do for him just in order to keep the peace within the house. See what I mean?
PG: I think so.
FATHER: We praise him when he does something by himself without being told to. But at the same time, when he throws one of his little temper tantrums to get someone to do it for him, we totally ignore him until he does it for himself. [*At this point Dennis gets out of his chair to pick up a pencil I had dropped, and hands it to me.*]
PG: [*To Dennis*] Thank you.

It is extremely interesting, to say the least, that Dennis demonstrates his helpfulness just when his father is criticizing him for always trying to get others to do things for him. I feel that it is crucial to acknowledge his helpfulness, for the reasons that have been discussed (to facilitate more acknowledgment by his parents in the future and to keep his options for giving open).

FATHER: [*Continuing*] We explain that with the energy he expended, and the time he expended to throw his little tantrum, he could've been done and onto something else.
PG: Um hum. What's your view of this, Mother?
MOTHER: Yeah, I know I'm not supposed to do for him. [*As*

his mother speaks, Dennis sits very close, placing his head in her lap.] I give in to him at times, when he has a fit — but then at other times I let him go. I've had enough fighting in my life. You get to the point in your life that you've been through so much that you've had enough of that. You're tired of it. Because it affects one person, and you don't know how to fix the other person. It affects me inside. It makes me feel bad, makes me really feel low and depressive. Which it does. Dennis has to understand that. He knows when he takes a fit. And at times I don't give in to him, but when I do give into him, then his father gets upset. And you know, he feels that any break that I give to him isn't right. I know. I understand that.

Dennis's mother refers both to her previous attempts to help her mother and how she has become worn out with the efforts involved in doing so. She also dramatically articulates the ways in which her own past difficulties make it difficult for her to hold the line with Dennis, acknowledging that her tendency to give in to Dennis when he has a temper tantrum may not be in his best interests.

PG: Um hmm.
MOTHER: It's hard for me. It may take a while.

This comment, combined with her previous statement "I know I'm not supposed to do for him," suggests that Mrs. S may have taken too much responsibility for Dennis's behavior on herself or that Mr. S has parentified her by blaming her for Dennis's behavioral difficulties. I do not wish to contribute to this possible parentification but to try to draw attention to her efforts to give to Dennis, to be helpful to him.

PG: Is part of this that maybe you feel badly that Dennis has had some difficulties growing up?
MOTHER: Yeah.
PG: You feel like you kind of want to make it up to him?

I empathically take Mrs. S's side while helping her to make a change toward expecting more of Dennis in a way that will facilitate his development. The emphasis is on creating opportunities for her to facilitate Dennis's development, in this case by helping him to do more and to be more responsible.

Later in the session, more information related to the ways in which Dennis's mother has been badly hurt emerges.

MOTHER: I can't have any more children. I had to have my tubes tied after Dennis because I had a very bad problem.

PG: I see.

MOTHER: I can go and have a reversal, a tube reversal. I've already seen a doctor about that. But my family doctor figures with my health problems it would be best that I don't because it would be a strain, you know, on my health and on the baby and me. But we have adjusted to it. Yeah, there have been times I've sat and thought, I wish I could have another one, for Dennis's sake. And for my sake and my husband's.

PG: [To Father] I wonder about that, from your side, if that's a disappointment for you.

FATHER: To a certain extent, sure.

MOTHER: Oh, it still bothers me at times. I lost two babies before Dennis was born.

Here is yet more evidence regarding how Mrs. S has suffered in her life, more possible justification for treating others inconsiderately if she chose to, and more reason to be impressed with her capacity to give to others.

MOTHER: My mother, I love her to death. And I was always the one who stuck by her and always the one who did things for her and took care of her. And she didn't see those things.

Mrs. S did a great deal for her mother despite having been treated badly by her; her mother's refusal or inability to recognize and acknowledge her care and consideration is a source of profound hurt.

MOTHER: I told my husband he's so lucky to have both of his
parents. You don't realize it till one's gone. It still bothers me.
I know my dad is probably at rest in his mind, to see that
things have gone well for us. I know if he were alive, that he
would, you know, he would love my husband. He would love
him. Once they're gone, that's it. That's why it bothers me,
the problems I keep having with my mother. And it bothers
me the way my mother has tried to use Dennis to get back at
me. Dennis. It seems like all the way around the only one
who's getting hurt and has gotten hurt is this one [*gesturing
toward her son*]. He's the one who got hurt. I figure, he's
gotten hurt mentally. Mentally hurt.

As I listen to this I am again impressed by how much sensitivity Mrs. S shows toward Dennis under circumstances that would
lead many others to think only of their own pain and hurt. It
also appears that she may be talking about her own mental pain
as well.

PG: As I listen to you, you've been hurt too.

I acknowledge past hurt.

MOTHER: Oh yeah. Oh yeah. I don't want him to get as hurt
as I've been in my lifetime.
PG: You've had a lot of losses.
MOTHER: Oh yeah.
PG: Just one thing, I can't help wondering, the overprotective-
ness that you notice . . .

Here, I am building on previous statements about her difficulty in setting limits and so forth, and yet taking a resource
orientation, emphasizing the caring as opposed to a "failure" of
some sort.

FATHER: Yeah.

PG: This would be a natural result of so many losses. Losing babies.

FATHER: [*With a challenging edge in his voice*] Is it? I don't know.

PG: Does it seem to you that perhaps that's part of the reason? That his mother maybe wants to treat Dennis as if he were a baby sometimes?

MOTHER: Oh yeah. I stand back and look. See how big he's getting. I look at pictures. He's really getting big.

PG: And he can do a lot of things.

MOTHER: Yeah. I mean, here he's doing okay, and I'm thinking, in five years he'll be 15. And I know he'll be standing at least six feet tall.

PG: Mm hmm.

MOTHER: And that I'm going to think back, ohmigod boy, I remember when you were a little baby.

DENNIS: [*Murmuring*] A little baby [*placing his head in his mother's lap*].

MOTHER: I remember this, yeah. Ummm. It doesn't take long for them to shoot up in years.

PG: And it is hard. You understand I'm not saying it's good to be overprotective. I think it can be hard for many people to watch their children grow up and to realize that now they can do things they couldn't do before.

I acknowledge the good feelings that parents experience when they can do things for their children and the natural difficulties that many parents have in adjusting to a child's emerging independence.

FATHER: [*Quietly and gently, looking at his wife and smiling*] Basically what's happening is that Martha, being so kind and spoiling everybody, that Dennis has come to expect it.

Mr. S has been critical from the first of what he sees as Dennis's tendency to demand too much; he has also been impatient with his wife's tendency to give too much. In this session I have tried to highlight the possible historical reasons for this. It appears that this discussion has been at least somewhat successful in helping Mr. S develop a more sympathetic and positive view of his wife's tendency to overgive and inadvertently infantalize Dennis. Here he boils his concerns down to their essence; that Dennis is acting as a much younger child would and is unnecessarily dependent upon his mother to do everything for him. Mr. S's tone in saying that his wife is "kind and spoiling everybody" is one of appreciation, not criticism; he values her kindness and generosity. The nonverbal communication that accompanies this statement makes it clear that he includes himself in the "everybody" and that he acknowledges her giving as positive. At the same time he continues to be concerned that Dennis has become too reliant on his mother's nurturance, that he has not learned to do things for himself.

SESSION 4: ONE WEEK LATER

In addition to the continuing overall goals, this session has two specific goals:

- To give Mrs. S an opportunity to talk about any feelings of disloyalty she may feel after having spoken critically of her mother's involvement in her life
- To learn about Mr. S's family of origin and childhood

PG: How has school been this week, Dennis?
DENNIS: Fine.
FATHER: His grades have been great. He brought home an A on his report card.
PG: That's great. It must feel good.
MOTHER: I'm proud of him. Because in the last few years he's

come up from Ds to Bs and I'm really proud. Really am. He still gets his moods in the morning and doesn't want to get up, but he gets up.

This is yet another illustration of Mrs. S's ability to both see and acknowledge her son's achievements and efforts (i.e., her capacity to rely on constructive entitlement).

PG: Have you been getting yourself up?
DENNIS: [*Looks inquiringly toward Father, but does not speak.*]
FATHER: The man asked *you* a question, not me.
PG: Have you been waking yourself up in the morning?
DENNIS: Yes.
FATHER: [*Firmly but without anger*] Tell the truth.
DENNIS: No.
PG: No.
MOTHER: Mommy comes and wakes you up don't I?
PG: I don't remember. Does Dennis have an alarm clock?

I ask about an alarm clock as a way of introducing a possible practical solution to the problem of getting up for school without presuming to tell Mr. and Mrs. S what to do, something that would rob them of an opportunity to do something to help Dennis themselves.

MOTHER: No. He doesn't have an alarm clock. I don't know if he would get used to getting up with one, because I have a radio clock that I don't use that he could use. He's asked me a couple of times, you know, "Mom, whose is that?" you know, "Is that yours? Are you using it?" That would be a good idea, for him, you know, but there are three people in my family that were hard to get up, my three brothers, and he takes right after them.
PG: I wonder if . . . Dennis, would you enjoy that? Having . . .

if Mom thought it would be okay for you to use that clock radio?

DENNIS: Yeah.

PG: Do you have a favorite radio station?

DENNIS: [*Shakes head "no."*]

PG: But you would find one?

DENNIS: I don't like any.

PG: Hmm?

DENNIS: I don't like any.

PG: You don't like any. But you would like to use the clock anyway.

DENNIS: Mm.

FATHER: My question is, Would you leave it alone?

DENNIS: Yes.

FATHER: Not play with the buttons and change the time. You hear me?

DENNIS: Yes.

MOTHER: Dennis likes to play with buttons. I guess that they, you know, play with the computer at school. One teacher, Mrs. Little, was telling me they have an Apple II they let them work with, and Dennis has worked with it at times.

DENNIS: I've only used it twice, that's all.

MOTHER: Well, you'll work with it more. I guess other classrooms use it, don't they?

DENNIS: Uh huh. And like, uh, computer lab have lot of computers.

MOTHER: Uh huh.

PG: You know, I was just thinking . . . looking over my notes here . . . we've talked about so much, and you particularly have talked so much last time, some very personal things.

MOTHER: Yeah.

PG: Things, I'm wondering, do you regret anything that you may have said?

The question is asked in case Mrs. S feels that she may have been disloyal in talking about her family, especially her mother's emotional problems and her difficulties with her mother. I have adopted a general procedure of asking this or a similar question following any session during which someone has, perhaps for the first time ever, discussed aspects of their family's past or present that may be seen as shameful or overly critical. While Mrs. S's statement that she has no regrets is typical, instances of regret are frequent enough that I have continued to ask the question.

MOTHER: No. Not really. Saturday I went to the doctor, my family doctor, Dr. Robinson, he asked me how Dennis was doing, how many times he talked during our meetings, and I told him. And he said that's good. He said, "I know you probably discuss a lot." And, he said it's best, you know, to bring out everything, you know, even if things are hidden there, you know, things that bother you that never have been brought out. But, he told me he hasn't seen Dennis in a while, you know, but, I guess the next time he does see him, he'll probably notice some change in him. Dennis did a no-no the other day when his dad came home from work. About the door?

Dr. Robinson clearly plays an important role here; his reassurance and support for the therapeutic process are significant enough that Mrs. S reports on them. There is no question in my mind that criticism or denigration of the family's involvement in therapy on his part would severely undermine the process.

DENNIS: Um. I forgot lock the door.
MOTHER: After you came in. What did we tell you? What have we told you? When you come in from school and Daddy comes in a few minutes after you?
DENNIS: Lock the door.
MOTHER: What happened?
DENNIS: I forgot lock it.
FATHER: And what else?

DENNIS: And no people allowed in.
FATHER: And who was in?
DENNIS: Mike. My friend.
PG: Did you forget?
DENNIS: Uh huh.
PG: Do you have, um, a little sign or something—a reminder by the door?

This intervention is similar to my question about an alarm clock—drawing attention to the possibility of practical solutions to concerns about Dennis's behavior without undermining his parents' options for giving to him.

MOTHER: No. We've just told him that on days when his father comes home late nobody's allowed in. Dennis and Mike are very good friends. The best of friends. But when they get together they're rowdy.
FATHER: They're 10-year-old boys.
MOTHER: Like any two kids.
DENNIS: Uh, Mike, 9. Ten, I. Mike's 9, I 10.

It may appear that little attention has been paid to Dennis up to this point, that most of the talk is among the adults present. Some readers may wonder why he was not dismissed at an earlier stage. Others will notice that he is not often the direct center of attention; neither his parents' nor the therapist's. This is not unusual in contextual therapy since our goal is to help parents in their efforts to be more sensitive to and considerate of their children's developmental needs, not to instruct them in how to behave, and certainly not to become the parent figures ourselves.

Focusing inordinate amounts of attention on a young child may, in fact, constitute a form of parentification. This is something that may be necessary in the early stages of therapy with many families, and may even need to be extended into the later stages of therapy with some families. From a strictly theoretical perspective we wish to avoid contributing to *any* further parentification of children. From a practical perspective, however, we may have the choice of implicitly or explicitly agreeing that we are "treating" the child in order to ensure the parents' involvement in therapy and so the continued opportunity to help both parents and child.

Contextual therapy with this family stands in contrast to some approaches that might dismiss the child early on to focus on the couple's functioning, one parent's individual psychological issues, or one of several parent-training paradigms. There are a wide variety of perspectives on the question of whether or not to include young children in family sessions. At one extreme are those who feel that any semblance of privacy, typically referred to as "family secrets," represents the devil incarnate and must be exorcised by enforcing a rule of complete inclusion of all family members, refusing to permit any private meetings, or even private telephone calls, with the therapist. Those who follow this line of thought may also believe that all children, even the youngest, already know everything, including the most intimate details of their parents' lives, and so should be present when discussions of these matters take place.

At the other extreme are those who believe that any problems experienced by the children, whether outwardly emotional or behavioral, are manifestations of marital discord as well as of children's efforts to take care of their parents' emotional problems and needs. Based on the assumption that children have already done enough, and in most cases far too much, to try to help their parents and perhaps to save their marriage, these therapists may routinely choose to dismiss children after the first family session and work with only the parents from then on. This is not the place to debate the merits and demerits of these two therapeutic stances; to the best of my knowledge there is no empirical evidence favoring one over the other. I simply wish to use these extremes to anchor the attitude of contextual therapy, or at least of this contextual therapist, toward the question of whether or not to include young children in sessions.

These decisions are made not only on a case-by-case basis but also on a session-by-session basis and in ways that are consistent with the core emphases of this approach: being partial to all those who may be affected by what happens in therapy, catalyzing opportunities for people to achieve greater balance in their closest relationships, and facilitating acknowledgment of people's difficulties in life as well as their efforts to give to each other. These principles make it impossible for a contextual therapist to adhere to any rigid rule regarding either the inclusion of children in all sessions or their exclusion from them. The principle of giving room to people to make choices themselves, benefiting from the therapist's guidance and suggestions but not being limited by them, leads to a dialectical approach to making decisions about whom to include in sessions. The therapist may suggest, she may raise issues (e.g., "Do you think that your children would benefit from having a chance to talk about what is on their minds?" "Do you think that your going into detail about your illness in front of your children might make them even more anxious?" "Is this something that might be easier to talk about in a private session?"), but she is much less likely to insist on anyone's participation or to refuse to let anyone participate.

I routinely invite parents to include even their youngest children in initial sessions and do not routinely dismiss children from subsequent sessions. Neither do I insist that they participate in all sessions, and may suggest that they stay at home under some circumstances. Examples of the latter would include planned discussions of sexual problems, serious medical problems, or actual or planned legal conflicts between a custodial parent and the child's other parent.

Up to this point Dennis has been relatively quiet in therapy, but the following exchange illustrates the benefit to him, and quite possibly to his parents as well, of his continuing presence in our meetings. It may also address the concerns of some readers regarding the capacity of a young child, especially one with such a significant cognitive impairment, to participate in and benefit from this form of therapy.

MOTHER: Then, when was it—last week—he called me up at work. He was upset. Um, tell the doctor why you were upset when you called me up.

DENNIS: What? I tell you this?

MOTHER: About your friend.

DENNIS: Yeah.

FATHER: You didn't tell me.

DENNIS: I coming home from school. Me and Ben. Best friends. Leaving somewhere, um, living somewhere else. By Memorial Park. And, uh, go home, running, and I call my mom up.

MOTHER: He was very upset. He was crying.

PG: Your friend was leaving.

MOTHER: His best friend, his best friend at school, had moved. And he called me up. And he was very upset, crying. I told him to slow down, calm down. He told me. And then when we got home, we found a phone number and they gave us the new one so he could call. But he realized, I guess he's starting to realize when you lose a best friend, how it feels. You know. Because he was really upset because my manager answered the phone and he said Dennis sounded upset.

PG: It is hard.

MOTHER: When you lose a friend.

PG: It's one of the things we were talking about last week.

MOTHER: Mmmm hmmm. [*The reference here is to Mother's own losses in the past.*]

PG: [*Following an intervening discussion on another topic, turning to Father*] We have talked some about your wife's family and I'd also like to know some about your family.

I am being partial to Mr. S by showing interest in his family and by providing an opportunity for him to talk about his early years.

FATHER: What would you like to know?

PG: Well, just to start off with, the names of your brothers or sisters.

FATHER: I have three sisters and one brother; I'm the oldest.*

PG: And your parents?

FATHER: My mother's name is Elizabeth. Everybody calls her Liz.

DENNIS: I call her Grammy.

FATHER: Well, she's your grandmother.

DENNIS. Uh huh.

PG: How old is your mother?

FATHER: Next birthday she'll be 59.

PG: And your father?

FATHER: They'll both be 59.

PG: They're both 59.

DENNIS: 58.

PG: Well, you're right and I wrote 59.

Acknowledging that a child is correct on a point of fact when I have been incorrect takes on added significance when the child is laboring under the limitations of cognitive delays and has been blamed for not doing anything for himself.

DENNIS: [*Mumbles something that to me appears to indicate interest, but that has a different effect on his father, who is extremely sensitive when talking about his family of origin.*]

FATHER: Let me ask you a question, Dennis.

DENNIS: Huh?

FATHER: [*Quietly angry*] Let me ask you a question. When your mom was talking, you were nice and quiet. When she was talking to the doctor. Okay. How come you've got to make comments in the background when I'm talking?

---

*Discussion of brothers' and sisters' names, ages, marital status has been deleted; discussion of his parents has been edited and condensed.

Dennis has been blamed for his behavior, where he should have been acknowledged; he has been parentified by his father who appears to need Dennis's attention as a form of validation of the importance of his statements. I strive to raise Dennis's side, the side of resource, without alienating his father, and while being sensitive to his father's feelings. To do this I acknowledge the possible impoliteness, while trying to cast light on the caring inherent in Dennis's interest. While the principle of multidirected partiality does not require that the therapist take more than one person's concerns into account at one time, such simultaneous side taking is occasionally possible, especially when working with children and their parents.

PG: I think that's a good question. Because, on the one hand, you might say, he's being, oh, I don't know, impolite, or
FATHER: [*Chiming in forcefully*] Impolite.
PG: Impolite. On the other hand, something occurred to me— I don't know what you think of this—maybe his comments are his way of showing that he's interested in your story.

In asking if Dennis's mumbling may actually reflect interest in his father I am able to acknowledge Dennis's giving and simultaneously Mr. S's importance as a father; this may help Mr. S to acknowledge his son's efforts to give in the future. Raising Dennis's side and emphasizing what appears to be Dennis's positive motivation also exemplifies the resource orientation of the contextual approach. It may or may not be taken as an example of a reframe, depending on the reader's definition of this term (as discussed at some length in chapter 3).

FATHER: Ask him.
PG: Is it interesting to you to hear your dad talk about when he was a little boy like you?
DENNIS: Yeah.
FATHER: Yeah.
PG: Is there something you want to ask him about it?

DENNIS: No.

PG: You just want to listen?

DENNIS: Uh huh.

PG: Do you want to tell him anything?

DENNIS: No.

PG: [*Turning back to Dennis's father*] What sort of a man is your father?

FATHER: Dad's a good guy—very mellow. Unless you get him excited, he's extremely calm. This is the only guy I know who can sit there and read the evening paper from front to back with global thermonuclear war getting ready to break out. That's how calm this dude is, I mean unless you get him excited. Then he can be just as wild as anyone else.

PG: When you think about you and Dennis, are you thinking that you'd like your relationship to be like what yours was like with your dad?

FATHER: Yeah. That wouldn't be a bad thing.

PG: Is it, is it like that?

FATHER: Mmmmmm. No. I would say not. Because the way he treats his mother at times is not the way that I treated mine. Which has an overall effect on our relationship.

Mr. S has just provided a crucial bit of information and a significant insight into the source of his impatience with Dennis.

PG: Are there other differences besides that ? Or is it similar in other ways?

FATHER: Oh. Very similar.

MOTHER: None of my brothers were close to my father. None of them, never really.

For the moment Mrs. S has slipped into the past, her husband's talking about his father bringing thoughts of her late father and her relationship with him to the fore.

DENNIS: I am.
PG: What were you saying, Dennis? You're close?

Here, I am being partial to Dennis by helping him to surface his concerns.

DENNIS: I miss my Pop-pop sometimes.
MOTHER: Oh. I know.
DENNIS: I miss him.
PG: You really do miss him. Are you sad, too, because your mom is sad?
DENNIS: No.
PG: Are you sad for yourself?
DENNIS: No.

It is a near certainty that Dennis is failing to comprehend my questions. If this can occur despite my best efforts to speak at an appropriate level, one can easily speculate about what may occur in the course of daily living, both at home and in school.

MOTHER: I don't know—Sometimes—I said to Bill last night, I asked about him and Dennis spending time together while he is at home in the evening because I go to work at four o'clock and I don't get home until ten. So I suggested that they do something. And then I said to him, "Well, we might as well enjoy the years we have left with him now." Because when he hits 15 I know Dennis's gonna be like "Mom, I'm going out with my friends." And this and that, you know.
PG: That's part of growing up.
MOTHER: It means a lot to me. I missed so many younger years with him because I always worked. I always worked and he was at the babysitter's.
PG: In a way it's hard to have him grow up so fast.
MOTHER: Yeah.
PG: And you know I ask a lot of questions. I don't claim to have all the answers. But I was thinking about the waking up.

MOTHER: Mmmm mmmm.

PG: That maybe one side of it is, you know, that if you had the alarm clock that would be easier.

MOTHER: Yeah.

PG: But, maybe there's a feeling of loss, too.

MOTHER: Uh uhh.

PG: If he doesn't need you for that, anymore.

MOTHER: Yeah.

PG: And that can be hard.

This is an example of being partial, in this case empathically so, to Mother, who is struggling to let Dennis grow up and yet is feeling the loss of the closeness that often exists between a mother and a very young child.

MOTHER: Yeah, mmmm.

DENNIS: Mmmm.

MOTHER: He does some things on his own. Yeah, that hurts me, you know, that bothers me some. You know, I think, yeah, this is my little boy growing up. I guess, you know, all mothers feel that way.

PG: I think so.

MOTHER: It's a different bond between a mother and a daughter. Mother and daughter, yeah. But a mother and a son, it's more clingy. You don't want your little boy to grow up.

In a few words this mother has encapsulated not only her feelings about her child's development, but also, perhaps, as she says, those of all mothers (and fathers too).

PG: You mean you're clinging to him.

Another example of multidirected partiality, one that involves both clarification and, to a certain extent, a measure of holding Mother accountable for her actions—in this case actions involving clinging.

MOTHER: Mmmm hmmm. I, you know, I look at him, and I think, god, he'll be 11 in two months. Next year he'll be 12.

PG: He's almost 12.

MOTHER: Uh huh. Yeah. My niece is. Um, girls — you don't really recognize growing up. I have a niece, she turned 15 years old today, and I remember when she was little.

DENNIS: Who? Beth?

This is another reminder that Dennis, while relatively quiet, is following the conversation very closely.

MOTHER: Sandy.

DENNIS: Oh.

MOTHER: And but, I'm thinking, when you really see a boy grow.

PG: They grow.

MOTHER: Yeah. And you know they're getting older. And you know he isn't my little boy any more. He's growing up to be a young man.

PG: When Dennis was a little baby, really, you needed to give to him a lot . . . and all he could do was take it in. The food and milk and be cuddled and all that stuff, and he needed it.

MOTHER: Yeah.

PG: He needed it. Now, maybe, Dennis needs to be able to give to you in some way.

I am offering Mother a way to continue to nurture her son by giving him opportunities to give to her.

MOTHER: Mmmm mmmm.

PG: And now he does it with his schoolwork. [To Dennis] It seems to me you like to give things to your mom and dad.

DENNIS: Uh huh.

MOTHER: It's a bond a mother hates to let go.

PG: I don't think you do let go, it —

MOTHER: I don't think you do let go.

PG: Perhaps it just changes.

MOTHER: Yeah, it changes.

I am trying to reassure Mrs. S that she can help Dennis and allow him to become more independent without losing the closeness she feels with him. Criticizing her for being "overprotective" would have been cruel, unproductive, and inconsistent with all the principles of the contextual approach.

PG: Dennis, do you have a comment?

Dennis is given the same opportunity as everyone else to contribute to the session.

DENNIS: No.

MOTHER: My stuff bore you?

DENNIS: Huh?

MOTHER: Does my stuff bore you that I talk about?

DENNIS: Nuh.

MOTHER: Huh? Do you get bored easy when I talk?

DENNIS: No. It's nice.

PG: Do you like it? When she talks about you? Mmm? You like that? [*Dennis does not respond. It appears that he has not understood the question.*]

PG: [*To Mother*] I just wondered, is that a form of giving, when he says it's nice. Does Dennis kind of know that will please you?

MOTHER: Mmmm mmmm.

I try the question again, this time making it as concrete as possible.

PG: You know that, Dennis? When you said, "It's nice," did you know that would make Mom happy?

DENNIS: Yes.

PG: You did know.

This is another example of the emphasis placed on acknowledging a child's spontaneous giving, and of the ways a therapist may help parents to notice their child's efforts to give to them.

[Later in the session]

PG: [*To Dennis's parents*] At home when Dennis wants to say something but can't seem to find the right words does he get angry, sort of mad at himself for not being able to express himself?

I am returning to the issue of the unfairness of suffering with a disability.

MOTHER: I don't know. I think maybe he does.
PG: May I ask him about this?
MOTHER: Sure
PG: Is that okay with you, Dennis, if I ask you a question?
DENNIS: Yeah.
PG: When you want to say something and you can't find the right word, and it's hard to talk about what you want to say, does that make you angry?
DENNIS: No.
PG: Does it make you mad?
DENNIS: No.
PG: No. How do you feel?
DENNIS: Good.

Dennis is perplexed by my much too abstract and hypothetical question about the causal relationship between his disability and his emotions.

PG: The reason I asked is that—not today—and I haven't seen it here—he participates very nicely—but the way you describe things at home, makes me wonder if he does get angry when he has trouble expressing himself, so I'm surprised at his answer. I don't know how you would see it.

Here my intention is to highlight how Dennis becomes frustrated due to language deficits. I do not wish to hurt Dennis and so refrain from belaboring the obvious—that he has misunderstood the question.

MOTHER: When he does get upset, I wish he would tell me, you know. And say something. Instead of just get mad and steam off.

PG: Do you see any connection between his difficulty with language and getting angry?

Again, I light the way for Mother and Father to acknowledge Dennis's struggles.

MOTHER: Mmmm mmmm. Um. He gets a lot of frustration.

PG: Frustrated. Maybe that's a better word.

MOTHER: Yeah. He will get frustrated, and when he gets upset and frustrated and angry but he won't come out and say anything, then a couple of seconds later he'll say, "You don't want me." You said that the other day, didn't you?

DENNIS: Uh huh.

PG: You think Mom doesn't want you?

DENNIS: No. She loves me.

PG: She loves you. So you just say that?

MOTHER: I think he just says that to see what my response is to him. And I told him, "If I didn't want you, Dennis, I wouldn't have you here. I wouldn't have cared for you, and done for you all these years."

8

LATER SESSIONS WITH THE S FAMILY

By the end of the fourth session many issues have emerged and been addressed in a preliminary way. In sessions 5 through 12 we continue to see changes in the ways Dennis's mother and father see and respond to him. Mr. and Mrs. S's continuing efforts to address their son's limitations appropriately as well as his increasing capacities for independence continue to figure prominently. Finally, Mrs. S's efforts to make sense of her relationship with her own mother continue as well, at times on the surface, at times submerged beneath it. These sessions continue to be guided by the same general goals detailed on page 129. Delineating specific goals for these later sessions, would, however, be misleading; the specific foci are dictated by the family's concerns at the time of each session, by their shared and individual moods, and by the opportunities each session presents to advance toward the overall goals.

SESSION 5: ONE WEEK LATER

This session begins with a discussion of Dennis's school progress. Mr. and Mrs. S inform me that Dennis will receive a formal psychoeducational evaluation at school sometime during the next several weeks. Mrs. S then begins to describe a recent problem.

MOTHER: He still gets his moods about not wanting to do his homework.

DENNIS: I did it last night.

FATHER: After what? After one of your temper tantrums?

DENNIS: Mmm.

FATHER: We have put out over $200 in glasses for you Dennis.

MOTHER: Oh yeah.

FATHER: [*Beginning angry but controlled, raising his voice as he continues*] And you picked those glasses up and threw them down on the floor. Now if I'd done that my ass would have been following it down, I guarantee you that. People don't get you things like glasses and clothes and food just because they love you so much. It's because you need them, Dennis, and they want you to have them. I don't want you walking around and keep running into walls. That's not going to do you any good, you need the glasses. And you don't need to sit that far from the TV screen either. You know you take your glasses off and then you go like this [*squints*] and you have to back up? That's because you *need* those glasses.

It is useful to consider Mr. S's anger in the light of two contextual concepts. First, it illustrates one of the ways that an adult's loyalty to a parent can affect his interactions with his own children. It is interesting to note that here, as in other exchanges where Mr. S refers to his parents' mode of disciplining him during childhood, he is not in any way critical of how he was raised; he is instead emulating his parents' expectations and their responses to violations of those expectations. Mr. S's statement also shows how hurt and angry a person can be if he feels that his efforts to be helpful, and to contribute to another person's well-being, go unacknowledged. Mr. S is quite clear in saying that he has spent a considerable sum for Dennis's glasses because he knows that Dennis needs them. He had perhaps hoped for acknowledgment, or at least the pleasure a parent takes in knowing that his sacrifices have helped his child. Instead of commenting on this, I choose to wait to see how the conversation develops.

MOTHER: [*Quietly*] You have to wear them.
DENNIS: [*Mumbles incomprehensibly.*]

At this point I am concerned that Dennis may not be able to state his side of this effectively so I try to find a way to help him clarify his feelings about the glasses. My next question is based on the assumption that Dennis dislikes his glasses, perhaps that other children tease him about them, but that he has difficulty expressing his discomfort verbally.

PG: Dennis, just so I understand, you don't like your glasses?
DENNIS: I do like them.

This is a perplexing response: Does Dennis actually like his glasses, or does he not understand my question? One option would be to pursue this doggedly with Dennis but as with the earlier exchange I choose to wait to see where his parents are headed instead.

FATHER: It's part of his tantrum.
PG: What started the tantrum?

I do not wish to implicitly accept the notion that Dennis has tantrums for no reason. A question of this sort may reveal important information about the causes of tantrums, including those factors that are embedded in family relationships.

FATHER: He didn't want to do his homework.
MOTHER: Yeah, he had a tantrum. I was sitting on the sofa and I said, "Dennis come up here and I'll help you with your homework," but he didn't want to. He wanted me to come to

him but I didn't want to, so I didn't. He took a mood swing and a fit. And then I said, "Dennis put your glasses on," and he threw them down.

FATHER: [*Directing considerable anger toward Dennis and even more toward his wife*] And you threw your little tantrum and your mother *let* you eat in your room. Do you have a problem with my saying that Martha?

It becomes clear that Mr. S is as angry at his wife for what he considers to be her overly lenient approach to dealing with Dennis's demands as he is with Dennis's behavior. I speculate that the intensity of his anger reflects possible injury he incurred as a young child when his mother may have disciplined him not just firmly, but harshly. And yet I do not believe that he is ready to hear such speculations on my part. The greatest potential source of therapeutic leverage continues to be his genuine desire to help Dennis to grow, to be more responsible, and to become more autonomous. Similarly, the greatest current block to his capacity to act on this wish is his anger at not being acknowledged for the efforts he makes to help. I listen actively for opportunities to acknowledge these efforts and to help Mrs. S acknowledge them as well in order to help Mr. S be free to continue to make such efforts in the future and to increase his freedom of movement and his ability to give. Such opportunities do not appear immediately.

MOTHER: No. I would settle for one night. I would like to have one peaceful night of nobody carrying on. It's been three nights a week of outbursts.

FATHER: Yeah.

MOTHER: And I get tired of it.

FATHER: Do you think I don't?

MOTHER: I've seen outbursts for years that you have never seen.

FATHER: [*Raising his voice*] I don't care about years. I care about right now.

MOTHER: But I'm telling you this. I'm tired of them—

FATHER: [*Beginning to raise himself up from the chair in a very angry posture, pointing his finger at Dennis*] Then start to control him.

MOTHER: Yes—

FATHER: [*Interrupting*] But controlling him doesn't mean giving in to him.

MOTHER: But wait a minute. There are some times that they get me to the point—when things are bothering me now, I can't help what I'm going through. I am coping with it [*referring to current medical problems*]—

FATHER: [*Interrupting*] Fine. [*Quite loudly now*] Cope with it then!

MOTHER: But I am tired of outbursts. I am tired of arguments and of you two fighting [*gesturing toward her husband and son simultaneously*]. Yeah we argue [*indicating Dennis*] but five minutes later, it's like nothing ever happened. But you carry it on for hours and *stay* in that mood and I *hate* that mood.

FATHER: That's the way it is.

MOTHER: I hate it.

FATHER: [*Quite angry now, almost shouting*] Then don't get me started.

I let this heated exchange continue for some minutes in order to see if Mr. and Mrs. S will be able to reach a resolution themselves and to see if any opportunities for acknowledgment present themselves. At this point it appears that their discussion is creating a great deal of heat but relatively little light, so I intervene to try to shift the focus onto possibilities for positive change. More specifically I apply the principle of multidirected partiality by holding Mr. S accountable for his remarks, for his emotionality, and for the implications of both for his son's further development. I do not do this to criticize Mr. S, to protect Dennis from his anger during the session, or to unbalance the family system. My intention, rather, is to help Father redirect his genuinely positive intentions in ways that are more likely to actually be helpful to Dennis. I believe that he does want to help Dennis; I also believe that his statements in the past few minutes have not been helpful. Being partial to him means holding a mirror up so that he can see the futility of his present course and change direction. Unless this is done he will continue to become angry that his efforts do not meet with success or acknowledgment; the anger will fuel itself; the result will be a downward spiral of resentment, anger, and alienation for both father and son. On the other hand, if I can help Mr. S to see that his laudable goals can best be reached through some other means, and especially if I can provide an opportunity for Mrs. S to acknowledge his past and present efforts to be helpful, he will gradually be able to increase his reliance on constructive entitlement; he will be able to respond with greater sensitivity and consideration to his son's unique needs. And, as a natural consequence, he will receive the acknowledgment he seeks and deserves; both directly and verbally from his wife, and indirectly and nonverbally from his son and from an improved father-son relationship.

PG: [*To Father*] Could I ask you a question?

FATHER: Okay.

PG: You know I try to understand all sides as best I can. So one question I want to ask is, Is there some truth to what your wife is saying; that when you get upset it's hard for you to break out of it, that it stays with you for a long time?

FATHER: [*Still angry, but less so than a minute ago*] Probably. Yeah, sure. The simple solution would be to just not get me started. The easiest way to do that [*gesturing angrily toward Dennis*] would be to *come* to the dinner table and eat like the normal American family with one point two children and everything or whatever it is now. Instead of *throwing* a temper tantrum, *throwing* yourself down on the floor, *demanding* [*gesturing toward Dennis again*] to eat in your room in front of the TV.

MOTHER: TV is the worst thing for kids.

FATHER: [*Angrily, raising his voice*] And you haven't done a thing about it. You keep threatening to take that Nintendo away and it's still there.

MOTHER: I just haven't had a chance to take it away from him.

[Later in the session]

MOTHER: I know I'm not supposed to give in to him, and I have not given in to him. I have not. I was in a very good mood the other day, and then Dennis refused to eat dinner; he wanted to eat in his room and all that. He said he wasn't hungry. Then I said, "If you don't eat now then you'll bother me later." Am I right?

Mrs. S feels that she must justify herself to her husband, making the case that she has started to take a harder line with Dennis.

DENNIS: Yeah.

MOTHER: So I just said the heck with it, "Eat in your room." And I got so frustrated I threw the tea kettle. I said, "I've had enough." I've come to the point that I've had enough of things like that in my life. I'd like to see for once nobody get upset, cause when you [*to husband*] get upset you *stay* upset.

FATHER: Well good luck.

MOTHER: There are days that they [*indicating her husband and son*] get along and things are fine.

PG: [*To Father*] I don't know if from your side it feels like it's something you can control or not.

Having spent a few minutes closely following the exchange between husband and wife I want to direct Mr. S back to the issue of his anger. His initial response is in the form of an invitation to me to scapegoat Dennis.

FATHER: [*In a somewhat threatening tone*] What, you mean Dennis?

I believe that Mr. S is testing me through his verbal and nonverbal confrontation to see if I will back down, take the easier path and blame Dennis or continue to hold him accountable for his actions. I believe that it would be a betrayal of trust to fail to maintain the focus on his anger at this point.

PG: Your own internal reaction.

FATHER: [*Pause*] It's controllable. You can control it in one of two ways. Say the hell with it and just don't care, and let him go on about his business the way he wants to, which means in the long run we're just wasting these sessions to begin with.

On the surface this is an angry and confrontational response, and yet I still believe it reveals a sincere wish to help his son and to take advantage of the help that therapy can provide. In saying that letting Dennis "go about his business . . ." would amount to wasting the sessions, Mr. S implies that he sees value in the sessions, that he does not want to waste them, and that he wants to stay the course.

DENNIS: [*Mumbles something half under his breath.*]

FATHER: [*Directing his attention to Dennis*] Did I give you a chance to speak? [*Turning to PG*] Or I could flare at him and *make* him do what we want him to do inside the home and try to show some consistency. We've got one of two choices.

I am impressed at Mr. S's ability to listen and respond to my statements about his angry outbursts. It also appears that he needs me to reassure him that we are on the same side; that while I hold him accountable for his actions I am also able to give him credit for his goals. As has been true throughout this case, the purpose of acknowledgment, in this instance reassurance, is to help each person achieve greater reliance on constructive entitlement, here to help Father achieve greater freedom to give to his family.

PG: The need for Dennis to behave responsibly is clear. So I don't think there is any argument about that, not from Mother's side and certainly not from my side. I don't even think that Dennis would argue about it. Does it seem right to you, Dennis, that you should do certain things the way your parents want you to?

DENNIS: Yes.

In asking Dennis this question I am parentifying him to a certain extent, using him to reassure his father that I approve of his goals. I believe, however, that the benefits outweigh the risks and that this step will help Mr. S to be more understanding and to give more to Dennis in the future. I also hope that it will help Mr. S to hear my next question somewhat less defensively than might otherwise be the case.

PG: Might it be possible that the approach isn't working, that Dennis doesn't respond well to anger and that he might respond better to a different approach?

FATHER: [*To his wife*] Is there another way to get him to do what we want him to do without anger?

MOTHER: Either he'll do it or he won't.

FATHER: And what ends up happening to us if he doesn't?

MOTHER: You get mad at me.

PG: Is that what happens?

FATHER: I get mad at him. We get mad at each other, and he wins in the long run because he still hasn't done it.

[Later in the session]

PG: [*To Mother*] Even though it is upsetting to you when your husband gets very angry—

MOTHER: Yeah.

PG: —do you feel that basically his intentions are good; that what he is trying to do is to be helpful, to kind of shape Dennis up to grow up and to be responsible?

MOTHER: Yeah.

PG: So you can credit him for what he is trying to give to you and to Dennis. [*At this point Father is sitting upright, no longer angry, but listening intently.*]

I have simply opened a door for Mrs. S to acknowledge the positive motivations that underlie her husband's angry statements. The change in Mr. S's demeanor reflects the impact of this acknowledgment: For the moment he has been freed of the need to claim credit for his efforts by being angry; his wife's acknowledgment has allowed him to give up some of his reliance on destructive entitlement.

[Later in the session]

MOTHER: Now he knows, "I can't get Mom to give in to me the way she used to."

PG: This giving in. On one hand I suppose anybody would try to get other people to give in to them, to have their own way if they can. On the other hand, almost everybody wants to feel that they are making a contribution, at their job, at work, or at home. Do you think that Dennis might really want to do more but may not know how to do it?

At every opportunity I continue to raise the possibility that Dennis would like to do more, contribute more, help more if he knew what to do and knew how to do it. Just as his father has become angry, resentful, and reliant on destructive entitlement as the result of seeing no acknowledgment for his efforts, so too has Dennis fallen into a pattern of oppositional and disruptive behavior following a similar lack of acknowledgment.

This pattern is not unique to Dennis. Many youngsters whose

behavior is troubling to adults are reacting to a lack of acknowledgment of their efforts to be helpful to their parents and others
in their families. There is quite compelling evidence that at least
some of the children whose behavioral difficulties lead to diag-
noses of attention-deficit hyperactivity disorder, oppositional
defiant disorder, and conduct disorder have primary underlying
neurological or endocrinological problems. Many others, however, are free from any neurological or developmental problems
severe enough to cause their disruptive behaviors. All of these
youngsters, those whose problems reflect underlying neurodevelopmental difficulties, and those who are free from such problems, benefit from acknowledgment of their efforts to give. I do
not wish to oversell this idea; it is a sad truth that some youngsters have become so locked into relying on destructive entitlement that they are not at all likely to be responsive to interventions that aim at removing blocks to giving.

Those, like Dennis and Timothy (chapter 5), however, whose
capacity to care about others has not been destroyed by exploitation and injustice in their own lives, those who still have a
reservoir of trust in others, are in prime positions to benefit
from these interventions. Diagnostic considerations, tapping
only psychological features, are insufficient to differentiate those
disruptive youngsters likely to benefit from contextual therapy and those who are not. The features essential to making
such a determination are revealed only in a family interview
conducted in a way that assesses and highlights people's capacities to recognize and acknowledge each other's contributions in
the past and the present; an interview that focuses on the balance of giving and receiving in the family. An interview of this
sort will reveal that many of these youngsters have been scapegoated for behaviors that actually represent their efforts to be
helpful.

Here we see Dennis being unfairly blamed for mumbling
when adults are speaking; something that appears to be rude
but actually reflects his intense interest and caring. For this

reason I strive to point to times and places where his parents may be able to directly acknowledge both his limitations and his positive efforts. Later in the session the focus returns to Father's anger at Dennis for refusing to do as he is told; my asking about connections with childhood experiences highlights both loyalty issues and Mr. S's reliance on destructive entitlement as seen in his intermittent inability to see Dennis's positive efforts and unique needs.

PG: [*To Father*] Does that pattern connect in any way with anything you might have experienced growing up?
FATHER: In my family, if I didn't want to do something my parents would say, "Do it or else," which is the way *I* would handle it.

The impact of Mr. S's own childhood on his expectations and parenting style emerges again and again. As was noted earlier, statements of this sort manifest both his loyalty connection to his parents and his reliance on destructive entitlement in this area of his family life. The key to identifying this reliance is his temporary blindness to the fact that his son's capacity to understand what is said to him and to respond in spoken language is not what his was as a child; he is temporarily blind to his son's cognitive capabilities, developmental needs, and personal sensitivities. This is also a moment when an appreciation of individual psychological functioning is highly salient; it is one of the features that distinguishes the contextual approach from some classical systems therapies, those that tend to ignore or pay little attention to people's unique strengths, weaknesses, and personalities.

PG: Is it possible that sometimes the manner in which you present yourself, the way you talk to Dennis, might be kind of overwhelming to him? You're a big man, with a big voice.

I continue follow the principle of multidirected partiality in holding Mr. S accountable for the impact of his actions on his son.

FATHER: But I'm not always presenting myself in that manner though.

PG: No. But like what you did a few minutes ago.

FATHER: Yeah.

PG: Do you think that the strength of that might overwhelm him and make it hard for him to really hear the message?

This is one example of how issues related to patterns of family transactions, in this instance those related to communication, may be integrated with the contextual emphasis on fairness and acknowledgment.

FATHER: [*His anger beginning to return*] I don't know. Would it? [*Now quite confrontational and a bit sarcastic*] You're the *doctor*. Would it?

MOTHER: [*Reaches out and touches her husband on the shoulder*] Wait a minute, wait a minute.

PG: I'm the doctor, but you're the dad.

FATHER: Yeah, so?

PG: I'd like to know what you think.

Mr. S's anger suggests that he needs special acknowledgment at this point, something that is also apparent to Mrs. S and something that she responds to vigorously.

MOTHER: Now there are times when he'll ask Dennis to do something, he'll say "Dennis" and he'll say it in a different tone of voice and it will click for Dennis. But when he uses that *strong, bold* voice I can see the look in Dennis's eyes: "That's not the side of Dad that I know. That's the mad side of Dad."

PG: That's what I was wondering, if it might actually result in a little fear or anxiety on his part. I would just like to share an impression with you. That's a voice that I would think if you got your car repaired somewhere and you came in and said in that voice, "Do you mean to tell me that you are going to charge me that much for this little job?" that most guys would say, "Let me take 10% off for you, sir."

FATHER: Yeah.

PG: That's just my thought, so I'm not saying it's a bad voice. It certainly can be useful, but my question would be: Is it possible that the other voice might be more useful for Dennis, that it might make it easier for him to hear what you are trying to say? Because what you are trying to say is 100% correct.

In this excerpt the major technical challenge involved finding a way to confront Mr. S with the implications of his harsh behavior while still being partial to him. In this instance, as in most other similar instances, I used a series of leading questions to highlight fairness issues. At the end of this session Mr. S appears to be placated but the ultimate impact of the interventions is far from clear.

SESSION 6: ONE WEEK LATER

In this session the initial focus is on Mrs. S's very difficult relationship with her own mother, her recollections of her mother's breakdown and her continuing wish for closeness with her mother despite these problems. The session contains several examples of how a therapist may be partial to a person who is not present but who is likely to be affected by what happens during therapy. It shows how a therapist may endeavor to catalyze a process of exoneration. This session also contains an illustration of how a child can be put in a position of having to split his loyalty: For Dennis this means having to choose between being loyal to his grandmother and being loyal to his parents.

MOTHER: We were at church last Sunday morning, Dennis was behaving badly, kept trying to sit up in front next to my mother. He knows he isn't supposed to do that. He doesn't understand why I try to keep him from my mother. It's because my mother has ruined my life and his and it has taken me a long time to get over that. I just don't want him around her. I've come to that point in my life that I just don't want my son around her. I tried to talk to her last Saturday on the phone trying to straighten out things between us but it just got worse. [*As Mother talks about her difficulties with her mother her husband leans back in his chair, as if he does not wish to get involved in this dispute. Dennis, by contrast, gazes at his mother with intense interest.*]

PG: You did try.

MOTHER: Yeah I did.

PG: You would like things to be better.

MOTHER: Yeah, but they aren't, so I put it in my mind that things aren't going to get better. We're never going to speak and that's just how it's going to be. She's classified me with my brothers. She has classified all of us as dead. So if she feels that way, that's fine with me. I've told my husband that I want nothing to do with her. I mean it. It's terrible to say but that's the way I feel. I've tried. I've done things for her, but the more I do for her—it's got to be her way or no way. I've come to the conclusion, thoughts, and everything since last week that she's a mean, evil woman. I've loved her to death. Now she's got me to the point that I don't care what happens to her. Because when she told me that she classifies me dead, hey, I know you're not supposed to feel that way but what am I supposed to do? Just sit here and take things from her? She has threatened to go to court to take Dennis away from us, but she can't because she is unstable around children. [*She begins to reflect on her mother's past emotional difficulties.*] My mother had a nervous breakdown. I was younger than Dennis; I was only eight. My mother had a nervous breakdown from an accident. She was in an automobile accident and it wrecked her nerves. My mother freaked out one night. My mother literally freaked. She started going after me, my father, and my brother. She took a frying pan and hit my brother. [*To Dennis, who has turned to look directly at her after this comment*] Yes she did, Dennis. I'm telling you the god honest truth. So my father called Dr. Robinson. My mother is very domineering. She has messed Dennis up to where he feels he doesn't have to listen to me and that's why Dennis has these problems.

PG: Did your mother get help, any therapy?

In keeping with the principle of multidirected partiality I am concerned about Mrs. S's mother who, based on this recounting of events, appears to have very serious problems and to be in need of treatment.

MOTHER: Never, just medicine from Dr. Robinson. He sent her to a psychiatrist, but she wouldn't go; and then she took herself off the medicine too.

PG: I don't remember the circumstances of your mother's childhood.

Since Mrs. S's first statements about her mother's harsh treatment of her as a child during session 2 (pages 137–141) I have been alert to any opportunities that might facilitate a process of exoneration. Here I try to further this by expressing interest in her mother's childhood in the hope that this will foster similar interest on Mrs S's part.

MOTHER: Her father was a very strict man. Her mother was a very loving, nice person, but her father was strict. I wish my mother was more like *her* mom, but she was more like her father. He was very strict, if you didn't do things his way, there would be trouble. [*This statement leads to a discussion of her mother's early years and then a return to the earlier focus on her mother's apparent mental illness.*]

It seems that the word "strict" has special meaning for Mrs. S and it begins to sound like "harsh and punitive" to my ear.

PG: It sounds like your mother has had a lot of difficulties. Do you think even now that she would benefit from more help, perhaps a different medication and someone to talk to?

This is another example of taking the side of a person who is not present in the therapy session, who is unlikely ever to be present in a therapy session (although I would welcome this if she and Mrs. S were agreeable), but who will be affected by what happens in therapy. I see Mrs. S's mother as a person who has suffered much, who has obvious serious psychological difficulties, and who has no other advocate in the therapy session—for this reason I try to raise her side as a way of helping Mrs. S to see her side as well. I believe that Mrs. S's sadness and upset over her difficult relationship with her mother largely reflects her self-blame for the stagnation of that relationship. I also believe that if she can do more and give herself credit for doing more to try to improve the relationship and for trying to help her mother, she will feel very much better.

MOTHER: She would, if she would go to someone to get it, which she won't. Her attitude is that there's nothing wrong with her, it's everybody else who has the problem. Dr. Robinson would probably agree with us.
PG: Would it help to have a talk with Dr. Robinson about this?
MOTHER: If she doesn't want to help herself, I'm not going to help her. I've done too much trying to help her already. If she would ever talk to anybody [such as a therapist] it would only be to down me and my husband. She has already told me that if she talked with anybody she would tell them that I was a no-good, rotten mother. Dennis has told her things about us. Tell the doctor what you told Grandma about me and Daddy. Tell the truth, Dennis.

Based on what his mother reports here, it becomes clear that Dennis has been placed in a severe split-loyalty situation with his mother and father on one side and his grandmother on another. His grandmother has encouraged him to resist his parents' efforts at control; his mother has tried to keep a distance between him and grandmother. In this regard neither adult has been concerned about, or indeed genuinely aware of, Dennis's feelings or needs. Their bitter feelings toward each other, the residue of terrible hurt on the one side and apparent mental illness on the other, leave them temporarily blinded to the needs of this little boy who they both genuinely love, but whose needs have been cast aside in the face of the press of their pain.

PG: Does it seem that in some ways Dennis is encouraged by his grandmother to speak badly to both of you?
MOTHER: Oh yeah.
PG: And might that be one of the biggest problems for Dennis?
FATHER: You've got it. If she doesn't have total control and domination over another human being, she's just not happy. And she will tell Dennis to say anything in order to start friction in our family so that she can step in and be, quote, "the savior of the marriage," or "I'll protect him," or, "Do it this way."
PG: Could I ask Dennis about this?

Dennis is already caught between two people to whom he wishes to be equally loyal, whom he loves equally, his mother and his grandmother. I want to find a way to highlight Dennis's bind without increasing the pressure it exerts on him. By asking his parents' permission to talk with him about his grandmother I hope to avoid exacerbating this bind, as I would if I asked him to reveal information or feelings against their wishes.

MOTHER: Sure.
PG: Dennis, does it feel like your grandmother wants you to say bad things about Mom and Dad?

DENNIS: Sometimes my grandmother says cuss words.

PG: What about the other part; does it feel like you're supposed to say bad things about Mom and Dad?

DENNIS: I like my Mom and Dad.

Dennis may misunderstand the question, as he has in the past; or he may be trying to find a way to answer it without being disloyal to his grandmother.

MOTHER: But what he's saying is, is your grandmother getting you to say bad things about Daddy and me?

PG: I don't want to push Dennis to say yes or no because there's a difficulty there. It would probably be just as hard for him if he were to say bad things about his grandmother. For a child this can be a kind of a bind, because even though his grandmother says some very hurtful things, is it possible that there is still a connection between Dennis and his grandmother?

I would like to help Mr. and Mrs. S see that they are contributing to this bind; to see that they are parentifying Dennis in order to gratify their own needs to blame his grandmother for some of their problems. While it might be tempting to direct them to stop doing so, such an intervention has a very low probability of success. It also would carry with it the problem of usurping their right to give to Dennis by spontaneously freeing him from the bind themselves; if they change their behavior only in response to my direction I earn the credit for the change, not they. For all these reasons I try to call *their* attention to the problem so that they can resolve it rather than trying to resolve it myself.

FATHER: The only connection I can see is that she wants to control his life and dominate his life and to take that control away from Martha and me.

This statement comes straight from Mr. S's being dominated for the moment by a reliance on destructive entitlement; he is so sensitive to, and hurt and angered by, his mother-in-law's behavior, that he is temporarily blind to the love his son feels for his grandmother.

PG: Do you think it's possible that despite all this Dennis feels some bond?

FATHER: [*Very angry*] Of course there's a bond there. What it *is*, I don't know, because he runs the place. He *runs* her life. She'll get him anything at all. If she gets him angry, then he wants to come back to Mom and Dad. She has literally tried to buy him through gifts and anything else.

PG: That's awfully hard for any child to say no to.

FATHER: Sure, he figures, "Hey, I've got it good here, I get everything I want, why should I go home and listen to those two people?"

PG: So what you're saying is that Dennis is caught because no child can say no to gifts and being a little spoiled, children love that, maybe a lot.

FATHER: Yeah.

PG: So for us to expect Dennis to say no would be crazy. On the other hand it seems that the cost of all those things might be that he has to choose sides, that he has to choose against Mom and Dad.

MOTHER: Yeah.

FATHER: That's exactly what the cost is. That's why I said she's literally trying to buy him, to buy his affection and his love, as superficial as it might be at that particular moment. It's gotten to the point now that everything is fine with Grandmom as long as he gets everything he wants. The first time she says no it's, "I want to go back to Mom and Dad."

PG: Do you think that in the future it might be possible for grandmother to see that doing that could be harmful to Dennis?

MOTHER: I told her Saturday on the phone that Dennis has to

start doing things for himself. She said, "Well he can't get up and cook on the stove all by himself." I said, "No, that's ridiculous, but what I mean is, he's got to dress himself, he's got to get up and pick up his own stuff. If he wants something to drink, go and get it. If he wants a sandwich, go and make it. Little things that he can do, that a kid can do on his own."

Mrs. S is working hard to place more age appropriate expectations on her son and would like her own mother to support her in this effort.

FATHER: Normal activities for a 10-year-old.
MOTHER: I said, "Mom you wait on him hand and foot, you give him everything. Why should I let you see him when we have been going to the doctor with him and getting him this help, and he has to keep on going, and I see how he behaves when he is around you and how all our work is being" [pause]
FATHER: Undone?
MOTHER: "Undone." And she said she would see him no matter what, and I said, "No, when he would come home it would take me three days to straighten him out." My mom told me that he sat next to her on the sofa and wrote "kill, kill, kill" referring to his dad. And [turning to Dennis] that you hated me.
[As Mother recounts this incident Dennis covers his face and turns his whole body to face the wall as if in intense shame.]
MOTHER: C'mon turn around. Don't get upset. Don't get upset. This is what you're supposed to have said. [Dennis turns part of the way around, but continues to avoid looking at his mother, father, or me.]
FATHER: She said you said it. Did you say it?
DENNIS: [Shakes his head.]
FATHER: Okay fine. That's that then.

Mr. S, in full fury moments before, is able to back off in the face of his son's obvious shame, remorse, and confusion.

PG: On the one hand Dennis is trying to do more for himself, and it's making him feel good, and you want him to have those opportunities.

I want to acknowledge Mrs. S for giving Dennis opportunities to be more independent, and to engage in developmentally appropriate activities; I also want to give Dennis credit for what he has been doing. The psychological reinforcement value of such acknowledgment cannot be denied; the more fundamental goal, however, is to catalyze a chain reaction that leads to everyone in the family having greater freedom to give to each other and to acknowledge each other's giving.

MOTHER: Yeah.

PG: On the other hand another major issue is this feeling that I think Dennis has about having to choose sides.

FATHER: Yeah.

MOTHER: I'm starting to do with Dennis what my brother did with his sons. He took his boys away from my mother.

FATHER: Just severed all contact with her.

MOTHER: They moved far away and everything. I could have done that, but no, I've been nice and let my mom see him. Now look what I've got, letting my mom see him and be around him has made me look like the bad guy. Now I feel like the further I am away from her the better off I am.

PG: Are you satisfied within yourself that you have made every effort to improve things with your mother?

MOTHER: Yeah, I feel a lot better.

PG: I was thinking about your mother and the breakdown and her other difficulties, her losing control that time at home. Do you think that in some way she might want to act better, maybe she doesn't even know that she wants to act better.

I have tried to take Dennis's grandmother's side at several points, here I continue this effort to acknowledge her suffering and raise the possibility that she might be more impaired than malevolent.

MOTHER: I don't think she can.

PG: Do you think that somewhere inside her is a person who would want to be more loving, more considerate?

MOTHER: Yeah. That's the Mom I haven't seen for over 10 years.

PG: If you feel that way, that inside she would like to be a different person, maybe there would be some benefit for Dennis if, as time goes along, you could help him to try to understand it. It's not an easy thing to understand, that someone deep down would want to do better but is not able to because they are not well.

My hope is that if Mrs. S thinks about how she might help Dennis to understand this, the process will be helpful to her as well, that it will lead her to a greater acceptance of the person her mother actually is, warts and all. Earlier, Mrs. S said that she wished her mother would be more like her maternal grandmother. If Mrs. S can allow herself to grieve over the loss of the mother she hoped for but perhaps never really had she may be better able to accept the mother she actually does have.

SESSION 7: ONE WEEK LATER

The session begins with Father trying to elicit information from Dennis. As this continues his frustration and anger at not being able to help his son communicate more effectively become evident. Mr. S's anger at not being acknowledged for his efforts to help Dennis is a continuing theme.

FATHER: Dennis, Do you have something you want to talk about?

DENNIS: No. [*Shakes his head.*]

FATHER: [*Angrily, but well-controlled*] Are you planning on sitting here for a year and not saying a thing?

PG: You seem angry.

FATHER: No more than usual.

Mr. S's statements and my responses illustrate how a contextual therapist may incorporate awareness of psychological issues such as transference into a therapeutic approach whose essence concerns the balance of fairness in real, rather than symbolic, relationships. Mr. S's verbal and nonverbal communication strongly suggests that at least some of his anger is directed toward the process of therapy and toward me as the therapist; the possibility that his remarks reflect the impact of transference must be considered.

Practitioners using an individually oriented psychodynamic approach might choose to focus on these symbolic or transference distortion aspects of Mr. S's statements. But recognizing the role of transference as a phenomenon does not force a therapist to talk about it as a transference distortion or as symbolic of another relationship. It is also possible to apply an understanding of transference by focusing on the implications of such statements on family relationships. Mr. S is unlikely to be comfortable with or respond well to questions or statements regarding how he sees me and our relationship. I choose instead to respond to him by asking about his expectations and feelings about the balance of fairness in therapy.

PG: From your side is there some question about the balance of responsibility, who should do what in the sessions? How much should Dennis be doing, how much should I be doing, how much should you be doing?

FATHER: What session is this? I think we're up to six or seven. How much *should* Dennis talk? [*To Dennis*] How much have you said to the doc?

A clear implication is "How much has the doc done to get you to talk?" Little would be gained by pointing this out to Mr. S at this point. I believe that my previous comment about responsibilities during sessions is sufficient and that further discussion of the transferential aspects of therapy would distract from the central goals, not contribute to them. I do, however, want to remain alert to helping Mr. S voice his opinions regarding his involvement in therapy, including any frustrations he may have about what he sees as a lack of progress.

DENNIS: Umm.

FATHER: Umm? How much have you said to the man? Do you want to talk about how you feel about certain things? Do you even want to be here? Why are we dealing with two different people? You're mister shy and innocent when we get into this room, but when we're outside of this room you ignore us. You throw your little temper tantrums and any time *I* say anything to you, you hide behind your mother's skirts. She can't turn around without running into you.

PG: The question you asked about wanting to come here is a good question for everyone. How are you feeling about that?

FATHER: [*Sarcastically*] Oh yeah, I enjoy giving up *my only day off* to come here with Dennis. But I'm sure none of us really want to be here, I'm sure you've got better things to do.

PG: Actually I'm glad to be here, but perhaps it's different, because it's my job.

This is a tricky moment: I want to make it clear that I am neither frustrated nor angry about the process of therapy, Dennis's level of participation, or Mr. S's complaints; in doing so, however, I want to avoid saying anything that enhances my worth at the cost of diminishing Mr. S's worth.

FATHER: It's your job. But we're here. And if we're going to get anything accomplished all three of us are going to have to participate in it.

PG: On the other hand I wonder if Dennis might be participating more than it might appear—by listening.

FATHER: When he wants to listen.

PG: How much do you think that is?

FATHER: Fifty percent.

PG: Why do you think he doesn't listen to the other fifty percent?

FATHER: Because he's bored or because he really doesn't want to be here; he'd rather be someplace else.

A sensible hypothesis would be that Mr. S is talking about himself here; that he is bored and would rather be someplace else. Many clinicians might decide to comment on this in terms of transference and with regard to the therapist-patient relationship. Contextual therapists notice and pay careful attention to all of a patient's communications, including those that reflect transference phenomena; for the most part, however, we choose not to interpret such comments with reference to the therapist-patient relationship, focusing instead on family relationship issues.

PG: Last week I shared some observations about the manner in which you express yourself to Dennis and I wonder if there is any connection between Dennis's shrinking away, something I see too, and the forcefulness with which you express yourself?

This illustrates one way of being partial to someone: Hold him accountable for the impact of his actions on others in a way that creates possibilities for positive change, in a way that has a genuine possibility of being helpful.

FATHER: When my wife expresses herself forcefully he doesn't shrink away.

This is a very interesting comment: For the first time Mr. S has acknowledges that his wife *does* express her wishes strongly to Dennis.

MOTHER: Children know that mothers are cream puffs.

FATHER: Are they? Obviously you don't know my mother.

This is Mr. S's third reference to his parents' firm approach to issues of discipline. Here he emphasizes the difference between his mother's style and that of his wife, illuminating our understanding of both his views on discipline and parental expectations and his tendency to be overly critical when his wife wants to handle things more gently than his mother would have. This brings up the possibility that Mr. S's invisible loyalty to his mother with regard to these parenting issues prohibits him from allying with his wife more strongly and supporting her more consistently.

MOTHER: You have that strong authority in your voice, and you always keep it, at least two thirds of the time. But that's the way you are. You can't change and I'm not asking you to change.

Of course by saying that she is not asking him to change, in fact that he can't change, she *is* challenging him to change. Whether we regard this as a paradoxical intervention by Mrs. S or not, it does seem to pique her husband's interest.

FATHER: What do you want me to do about it?
MOTHER: What can I tell you to do? I can't tell you to stop because you won't stop. You're over 30 years old and you're not going to change. But I want to say this. I think at times Dennis hears everything but he's afraid to respond. Because Dennis won't comment or say anything, and my opinion is that when somebody won't comment or say anything, it's because they're afraid to.
PG: Might Dennis be afraid of saying the wrong thing in here?
FATHER: I've never told him not to say the wrong thing or to be afraid of saying the wrong thing. At least it would be something.
PG: Do you think he might be afraid anyway?
FATHER: Why should he be afraid? We're only sitting here talking.

PG: That's right, but a lot of people are afraid of saying the wrong thing, especially children. That's really all I can say.

FATHER: [*Leaning close to Dennis, and speaking gently*] Dennis, how come you don't talk, buddy?

This represents a major change in Mr. S's approach to Dennis. Prior to this he was so locked into thinking of Dennis as oppositional and resistive that it had apparently not occurred to him that his son might be fearful.

DENNIS: I don't know.

FATHER: [*Not quite as gently*] You don't *know*? You have nothing to say?

DENNIS: [*Nods but does not speak.*]

FATHER: You have something to say? Am I bothering you by asking you a question?

DENNIS: [*Shaking head, mumbles*] No. [*He is clearly feeling badly; his eyes are downcast, his head is in his hand.*]

FATHER: Pardon?

DENNIS: No.

FATHER: Why are you wrinkling your brow like I'm bothering you?

DENNIS: [*Very quietly*] I don't know. [*Spoken very quietly. His mood appears to be even more gloomy. He is slumped down in his chair, head still leaning to one side and resting on one hand as if he needs the extra support.*]

FATHER: [*Increasingly exasperated*] You don't know. Is that your standard answer? [*At this point father turns from Dennis and faces PG. His body language suggests frustration with both Dennis's response (or lack thereof) and his own inability to elicit more from him. He looks at PG as if for an answer or for guidance.*]

PG: I could be wrong, but my own sense, just what you call a gut feeling—

FATHER: [*Impatiently*] Yeah?

PG: —is that there is some fear, some worry, not necessarily because you've done or said anything, perhaps it's just the mirrors and the camera, the whole situation.

FATHER: [*Crossing his arms, leaning back in his chair*] Try a session without me. See if he says anything at all.

PG: I don't think we should do that, because after all, no one can care about a child as much as his parents do, and when you come right down to it no one can help a child as much as his parents can. All I can do, if I'm lucky, is perhaps to be able to help a child's parents in their efforts to help their child. I can't change a child, and I can't care about a child in the same way that his mother or father do. That's why I ask you both to be here. And I suppose, just as a personal thing, it doesn't bother me as much when children don't talk very much. If we could look at videotapes of other families I think you would be surprised at how little most children say. When I ask a child a question and he says, "I don't know, maybe," that's a good answer, that's something. There are exceptions to that, but not very many.

MOTHER: I didn't talk much when I was a kid; I was always afraid, of my classmates and everything. It seems like Dennis talks to his classmates.

After hearing me give Dennis credit for what he does say, something that by extension gives her credit for being a good mother, Mrs. S lends her support to him as well.

PG: So Dennis is in some ways doing better than you did as a child?

By giving Dennis credit for doing better than she did as a child I am also giving her credit for being a better parent than her mother was.

MOTHER: Mmm hmm. Dennis didn't have a mother like I did. My father more or less didn't say anything. When he did, my mother more or less ignored it or gave him mouth over it.

PG: Maybe *he* was afraid of saying the wrong thing.

MOTHER: He was.

SESSION 8: FOUR WEEKS LATER

A two-week break had been scheduled between sessions 7 and 8. Mr. S telephoned to cancel that appointment because his wife was not feeling well; scheduling difficulties necessitated an additional week's delay. During our telephone conversation, Mr. S said that Dennis's behavior had improved considerably. He also commented that Dennis continued to have intermittent temper tantrums, but that this was "like any 10-year-old boy."

PG: How have things been going?
FATHER: From what I can see there has been some improvement compared with when he didn't come here, when we didn't have a session. But at the same time, a three-week layoff—we've seen him start to slide back to some of his old ways. [*Mr. S describes some specific examples of behavioral changes and then continues*] We've seen a big improvement since we started coming here.

This is, to say the least, a very interesting change from the tone of Mr. S's comments during the previous session. I never imagined that I would hear him complain that a three-week break from therapy was too long.

Dennis's parents are planning their first trip without him in ten years. The following discussion focuses on Dennis's difficulties in expressing his concerns about this. His parents feel that he is fearful but are not sure what the fears center on. His mother wonders aloud if Dennis fears that they would abandon him.

PG: May I ask Dennis a question about this?

I ask for their permission to broach the subject with Dennis, so that he may speak without worrying about saying more than his parents would want him to.

MOTHER: Sure.

PG: Dennis if you were afraid that Mother and Father would not come back, would you say so? Would you say, "Mom, I'm afraid you won't come back; Dad, I'm afraid you won't come back"? Would you say it?

DENNIS: No.

PG: Why?

DENNIS: Scared.

PG: Scared—of what?

DENNIS: Scared of saying it.

PG: Scared of saying it. You mean nervous?

DENNIS: [*Nods silently.*]

PG: Sometimes is it worth doing a thing that you are nervous about?

Here is another example of my being partial to Dennis by helping him state his side, and also to Mr. S, who desperately wants Dennis to communicate more fully with him.

DENNIS: [*Nods again.*]

PG: Did you ever do a thing that you were nervous about? Was there ever a thing you were afraid to do but you did it anyway?

DENNIS: [*Smiles and shrugs.*]

I want to find a way to give room to Dennis's mother and father to help him in some concrete way with his fear of putting his concerns into words.

PG: [*To Mother*] Was there ever a thing you were afraid to do that you did anyway that you would like Dennis to hear about, that might help him to understand?

MOTHER: Let me see. With my mom. If I did something with Dennis that she didn't approve of at times I was worried about it.

PG: It sounds like sometimes you also worry about how other

people will respond to you but you do what you think is right anyway.

MOTHER: Yes, I do.

PG: [*To Father*] Could I ask you the same thing? Is there something that you would want to tell Dennis that you were afraid of or nervous about that you went ahead and did anyway and you were glad you did?

FATHER: Something that he could understand?

I am acutely aware of Mr. S's need to find some way to help his son overcome, or at least cope with, his cognitive impairments. I invite Mr. S to share a personal experience with Dennis in order to provide him such an opportunity, an opportunity to help his son and so to increase his own self-worth; to build up his reservoir of constructive entitlement.

PG: Yes.

FATHER: [*Speaking directly to and looking directly at Dennis*] Have you seen the scars on my leg? After my accident? They said I might not walk again. I told them I would and I went ahead and did it anyway, but I was scared. I had to learn to walk a different way. You know how you walk?

Mr. S's fervent wish to do something to help his son has been evident throughout. I would like to be able to help him to do this rather than to address Dennis's anxieties myself. Here, when the topic at hand provides an opportunity, Mr. S responds strongly and clearly.

DENNIS: Straight?

FATHER: I can't walk like you. Have you seen me walking like this? [*Making a serpentine gesture to illustrate his point*]

DENNIS: Curved?

FATHER: Yeah. But I had to learn to do that. I had to learn to walk a different way. I had to learn to walk all over again.

All right. Believe me, I was *big time* scared of just getting out of bed and standing up on my legs.

PG: That's a great example. Do you understand what your father is saying?

DENNIS: Mmm hmm.

PG: So your father had to try something that even the experts told him he might not be able to do.

FATHER: Doctors with all kinds of degrees hanging on the wall said, "You'll probably never be able to walk again." I said, "Wrong answer."

This casts an interesting light on Mr. S's sarcastic comment in session 5, "I don't know . . . You're the *doctor*."

PG: What kind of accident was it?

FATHER: I was struck by a car. My right leg was crushed and they were on the border of deciding whether to amputate it or not. I have a steel rod in it, a new knee, and everything.

PG: But you walk.

FATHER: [*Turning to his son*] I'm walking now, aren't I dude?

PG: But it's hard for your father to walk. Does it hurt sometimes?

FATHER: Oh sure. [*To Dennis*] Do you know when I wear my brace and my special shoes? That hurts too, but I've got to do it.

PG: So maybe it was hard for your father to learn to walk again just like it's hard for you to talk. [*Dennis does not appear to be aware that I am talking to him.*] Dennis, it's hard for you to talk sometimes?

DENNIS: Mmm hmm.

PG: Do you think it is the same way for your father? Hard to walk sometimes? Would your father understand if you had to try really hard and maybe you didn't do it right the first time, or even the second time, or even the third time? I bet when he started to walk after the accident he couldn't do it the first

time he tried. Maybe he even fell down once or twice. [*Father nods in agreement.*]
PG: Maybe there were times he felt like quitting, like saying it's too hard. But he didn't.

Here, I am trying to understand and acknowledge the extent of Mr. S's trauma, at the same time trying to help him to use his experience to help Dennis. My fundamental goal is to facilitate Mr. S's efforts to be truly helpful to his little boy. It also presents an opportunity to help Mr. S see how painful and effortful it is for Dennis to put his experiences into words, just as it was for him to learn to walk again.

MOTHER: Do you understand?
DENNIS: Mmm hmm.
FATHER: Then say something. Were you listening to Doc?
DENNIS: Listening to some.
FATHER: Some?
PG: Do you think he understood?
FATHER: He understood the part of your statements he decided to listen to.
    [*Mr. S leans forward and faces Dennis. His posture and demeanor are nonthreatening, resembling the forward leaning posture of an empathic Rogerian therapist and in stark contrast to the judgmental and critical attitude manifest in earlier sessions. Dennis, attentive and smiling slightly, looks directly into his father's face. This also contrasts dramatically with Dennis's earlier avoidance of looking directly at his father in earlier sessions. Now speaking clearly and deliberately, without any trace of anger, he continues*] What we're trying to get across to you is, if you want to say something, *say it.* [*When Mr. S says "say it" he claps the back of his left hand into his cupped right palm, in a strong but nonthreatening gesture. Unlike his behavior in previous attempts to communicate with his son, he does not point at Dennis at any time.*] Give it a shot. So the words don't come out right? [*Mr. S turns very*

briefly to PG, making fleeting eye contact as if for approval, acknowledgment, or support.] You know when you get excited about something and you come to me, and you're saying "Umm, umm, umm" because in your mind you're looking for the right words? What do I do? [*At this point Mr. S is leaning forward toward Dennis, looking directly at him. Dennis continues to look directly back, smiling even more widely, and leaning a bit toward him as well.*] I say, "Slow down. *Think* about what you're gonna say, and then say it." [*Mr. S continues to gesture with his hands while he speaks, but as earlier in this exchange his gestures are illustrative rather than confrontational or threatening. He sweeps his left hand away from Dennis in an expansive gesture as he continues to speak.*] And that's all you've got to do about *anything* you want to say. Chill. [*Looking intently at Dennis*] Right, just chill for a second. Think about what you're going to say. If the words don't come out right, Hell, I'll get the *idea*. Mom will get the *idea*.

As this session progresses Mr. S continues to stress how important it is to him that Dennis make an effort to talk with him and to respond to questions regardless of any cognitive limitation that might interfere with complete success. He is particularly clear about his anger when Dennis responds to questions by saying "I don't know."

FATHER: I'm tired of hearing "I don't know." You *do* know.
PG: In fairness to Dennis, though, it does seem that there may be times when he really doesn't know.

I lend my support directly to Dennis. As we have seen repeatedly throughout this case and this book, the principle of multidirected partiality guides therapists to take the side of the person who needs it most at that moment — one feature that differentiates this approach from those that advocate being neutral as a way of globally caring about everyone equally.

FATHER: There might be *times* that he doesn't know. Okay.

PG: When we were talking earlier about what Dennis might be afraid of that keeps him from talking, maybe he didn't know.

DENNIS: I hate when people make fun of me.

PG: They make fun of you when you talk?

DENNIS: Mmm hmm.

PG: So it's better not to talk?

DENNIS: Mmmm hmm.

FATHER: How do you figure that?

DENNIS: Hmm?

FATHER: How do you figure that if people are going to make fun of you that it's better not to talk?

DENNIS: They call me names.

PG: What do they call you?

DENNIS: Umm, retarded.

FATHER: What people?

DENNIS: Some people.

FATHER: Yeah? Where?

DENNIS: At school sometimes.

PG: How do you feel about his school?

MOTHER: Dennis does really well there. He gets straight As in spelling. We should be getting some papers later this month for his evaluation. The psychologist who will do the evaluation at his school told me that the last time she saw Dennis she could see that he had improved a lot compared to last year.

DENNIS: I don't like music.

MOTHER: You like chorus though. He likes chorus, but he doesn't like his music class.

FATHER: Now you've been sitting here talking just fine with all of us. How come you don't do that at home Dennis?

Dennis is silent and seems overwhelmed. Despite my general belief that I can help more by facilitating communication than by leaping to someone's defense, I feel that Dennis needs my direct assistance at this moment.

PG: Dennis is very sensitive. And children are often much more concrete than we adults. They like things to be nailed down.

MOTHER AND FATHER: [*Simultaneously*] Yeah.

PG: So for us as adults, we can say, "Well we would like to help Dennis express himself more," and if he would both of you would be pleased and would say, "That's good." And that's enough for us. But maybe Dennis needs a concrete example to show him that people really do want to hear what he has to say. I know how pleased both of you would be; but I'm really not sure if Dennis knows.

MOTHER: I think he knows certain things to an extent, but not everything. If Dennis does something wrong, he gets scared. So I'll ask him about it and he'll get mad and upset. He'll say *I'll* get mad if he tells me, and I'll say, "No, not really, if you tell me what you've done wrong, I wouldn't get mad. No matter how bad it is, tell me." I think it's because of what he's been through. My mother always did all his thinking for him, which is over half of the problem. [*As Mother continues in this vein, Dennis forms circles with his index fingers and thumb on both hands, holding the resulting circles up to his face, one thumb-and-finger circle over each eye.*]

PG: Dennis, what's this? [*Imitating Dennis's thumb and fore-finger circles*] I'm sure it's something but I don't know what it is.

MOTHER: What is it, Buddy?

DENNIS: It's a face. It's a owl face.

PG: Owl face?

MOTHER: Where did you learn that?

DENNIS: My friend.

MOTHER: Your friend.

The owl face presents an opportunity to directly acknowledge Dennis's capacity to learn and to catalyze more acknowledgment from his parents.

PG: So Dennis can learn new things. And he can also learn a new way of talking about things. It will take some time; it won't be easy, but he can do it. [*During this exchange Dennis is particularly animated. He once again demonstrates the "owl face," and then begins to mime talking, complete with gestures he copies from me and his father.*]

FATHER: Well, he can talk very well now. When he wants to get an idea across and doesn't get excited about it, he can get it across. The words don't come across right or the pronunciation is wrong, but we can get the idea and repeat it back to him, "Oh yeah, that's it," and you know that's the first step.

PG: I just noticed Dennis was saying something.

FATHER: Go ahead.

PG: What were you saying?

MOTHER: [*Reaching out her arm to Dennis, she sounds amused but not disapproving in any way as she speaks to him*] What were you doing? You'll have to remember what you just said here.

DENNIS: What?

MOTHER: While your dad was talking? It's all on the tape, but what were you doing?

FATHER: Mocking the way I was talking?

Mr. S once again reveals his sensitivity to Dennis's responses to him; a sign that he has unintentionally parentified Dennis by looking to him for validation and approval.

DENNIS: [*Nods, smiling broadly and openly, obviously misunderstanding his father's question.*]

FATHER: [*Morosely*] Yeah.

PG: But why?

I am being partial to Dennis by helping him to clarify what he intended by his imitations of his father.

DENNIS: Don't know.

PG: Did it seem to you that your father was angry with you?

DENNIS: No.

PG: Did it seem to you that he was being mean to you?

DENNIS: No.

PG: Did it seem to you that he was being nice?

DENNIS: Yes.

PG: Then why were you imitating? You want to be like him?

The quality of Dennis's facial expressions, vocal intonation, and body language all suggest interest and a pleasant mood; they are not at all consistent with a smart-alecky mockery of a parent. My impression is that due to Mr. S's sensitivities, his personal psychology, he reads a critical intent into Dennis's actions when none is there. Thus, my question, one that may appear to be a desperate attempt at a reframe or positive connotation, is really nothing of the kind; I am simply trying to share my observation of what Dennis seems to be doing.

DENNIS: [*Grinning sheepishly, looks first at his mother, then at his father, then back at his mother.*]

MOTHER: Go ahead and answer, Dennis.

DENNIS: Yes.

PG: You want to be like him. [*To Father*] Is that okay with you?

FATHER: [*Obviously very pleased by this idea*] Not setting his goals very high is he? But [*pause*] that's fine with me.

Taking Dennis's side by pointing out what I believe he has been trying to do is particularly important here because misperception has upset Mr. S, made him angry, and perhaps humiliated him in a way he would be uncomfortable putting into words. A different take on Dennis's actions, one I believe to be more accurate, has the opposite effect: Giving credit to Mr. S for being a father worthy of emulation enables him in turn to be appreciative rather than rejecting of his son. This is a clear illustration of how acknowledgment advances a therapeutic process; crediting Dennis for emulating, not mocking, his father also credits Dennis as a good and loyal son, and his father, by extension, as a model parent. Having been acknowledged as a good parent Mr. S is then able to respond positively to his son, the anger and hurt that blocked his ability to give having been removed. At the end of this session Dennis's parents decide that since things have been going very well they will schedule the next session in two weeks.

SESSION 9: THREE WEEKS LATER

This appointment, originally scheduled for two weeks after session 8, was postponed due to Mrs. S's continuing medical problems. As this session begins, Dennis is slumped in his chair, looking particularly miserable. The reason for this soon becomes clear as his mother details her increasingly debilitating symptoms. The session highlights the way that serious personal problems can temporarily blind even a very caring parent to a child's caring, concern, and upset.

MOTHER: We've been doing alright but Dennis has been running off course lately. Last night he took a fit because he didn't like what I made for dinner. But instead of telling me, "Mom I don't want it, I want something else," he took a fit. Just like now he won't open that soda and he knows how to open it. He wants me to do for him, and I won't.

PG: You weren't feeling well last week.

Mrs. S's medical problems are a very significant concern. It would be unrealistic to expect to understand current family relationships without first learning about her current health status. The contextual model, unlike many other therapeutic approaches, pays close attention to issues of health and illness, incorporating them along with other objective aspects of individual and family history in dimension 1, often referred to as the existential dimension. As was discussed in chapter 1, this is the dimension that taps the objective, factual, aspects of a person's life, such as the circumstances surrounding one's birth, one's gender, ethnicity, and race, and of course one's physical health from conception onward.

MOTHER: Yeah. I wasn't feeling very well. I'm going to another doctor, a specialist on June 28th. That's as soon as they could get me in. They want to keep it from getting worse as much as they can. Well, they've been telling me all along that eventually I'll be crippled over this. I've got like 15 years before I'm in a wheelchair. And the doctor wants me to have different tests to see what they can do and what kind of medicine I should be taking for my circulation and my joints.

PG: Do you think that Dennis is worried about your health?

This may seem like the most obvious question in the world, one that hardly needs asking. And yet Mrs. S's distress is such that she cannot see — quite literally cannot see — that her son is very worried about her, that he is perhaps even afraid that she will die.

MOTHER: No, not really. To tell you the truth, no. The only thing that worries Dennis is that he might not get his way. When I get mad at Dennis he won't talk to me.

This is the one area where Mrs. S's physical discomfort and, more than that, her anxiety about the future is such that she relies on destructive entitlement; her concern about her physical well being is so immediate that she becomes temporarily blinded to the impact on Dennis despite the presence of obvious emotional signs. Because of this I once again voice his side.

PG: He looks like he's going to cry.

FATHER: He doesn't cry; he *whines*. He's a great actor; he'll probably win an Oscar.

At first Mr. S's remark seems almost unbelievably insensitive; as the session unfolds, however, the reason for this insensitivity becomes clearer.

PG: Dennis, I wonder what you think about Mom having been sick. Does she seem all better to you?

DENNIS: I don't know.

PG: What do you think? Do you think she's still sick or is she all better?

DENNIS: [*Continues to look very unhappy but does not speak.*]

PG: What would be your guess?

DENNIS: [*Eyes downcast, hand to forehead, and looking close to tears*] I don't know.

PG: When Mom talks about having to be in a wheelchair, does that worry you?

DENNIS: [*Nods vigorously.*]

PG: What do you think?

DENNIS: [*Rubbing his eyes and shrugging*] I don't know.

PG: Does it scare you?

DENNIS: No.

PG: Does it make you feel sad?

DENNIS: No.

PG: Does it make you angry ?

DENNIS: No.

MOTHER: You don't know how it makes you feel, do you, Dennis? The only way that Dennis knows that Mom is really sick is like last year when I was in the hospital with it. Because I was to the point last year that I could hardly walk right. But if Mom is home and Mom can get up and walk, then Mom isn't sick. Yeah, he seems like he cares and he shows it some, but not a great deal. No kid would at his age. Dennis cares about Dennis right now. Dennis worries about Dennis. But I feel cheated. I feel cheated. In 15 years I won't even be 50 and I'll be in a wheelchair. But I get up every day and I live with it. I've learned to go on. They say sometimes it runs in families. I wouldn't want it to happen to him. That's one thing I wouldn't want to happen to him because Dennis is a very active kid. It's hard, but I adjust to it. Now the other night when Dennis and I sat talking, he talked. For the first time in a long time he talked, but when he doesn't get his way on things he gets mad. He gets upset and he stamps off, goes up to his room and slams his door or something.

This is yet another example of Mrs. S's capacity to think of others even as she is acutely aware of the unfairness in her own life. As she says, she has been cheated. Although briefly unable to see or acknowledge the impact of her health problems on Dennis, here she spontaneously thinks of Dennis and hopes that he has not inherited her propensity for inflammatory disease.

PG: We've talked before about Dennis's difficulties with language. And we've talked before about how he does a lot better at putting his ideas into words when he's feeling good and how he does a lot worse when he's under stress and when he's upset. Do you think it's possible that he may be upset about your illness—

As I have many times in working with this family I try to put myself in Dennis's place, to speak for him, to give voice to what I believe may be his thoughts and feelings since he may not be able to.

MOTHER: But not know how to show it.

I am impressed by how Mrs. S is able to put her own concerns aside and to see Dennis's side of things.

PG: Maybe even within himself he may not know what to do with it.

FATHER: [*Angrily*] Doc, I really don't think he gives a damn. As long as Dennis is taken care of, that's all he cares about.

Father's anger, especially in the light of the concerns about his wife's health, is understandable and yet I feel it is my responsibility to challenge his apparent belief in Dennis's lack of caring about his mother. Such challenges, those that hold people accountable for both what they say and do, as well as for the impact of these statements and actions on other people, are intrinsic to clinical work guided by the principle of multidirected partiality.

PG: That's a harsh statement. Do you really believe that?

FATHER: You don't live with him. I'm serious. As long as Dennis is taken care of, that's all he cares about. As long as he can come home from school, ignore the rules we have set down and basically do what he wants to do, he's happy as a lark.

The conversation continues in this vein for some minutes, with both Dennis's mother and father pointing out Dennis's apparent lack of concern for them.

PG: Do you think it's just a coincidence or that there is more to it—that you got quite sick and the question of your illness became more here and now, not just in the future but right now. That's a stress on everyone. Knowing that 15 years in the future a wheelchair may be necessary is one thing.

FATHER: [*Confrontational*] Yeah. So?

PG: But seeing your wife in pain and partially incapacitated today is something else.

FATHER: When she is partially incapacitated today it's *our* job [*indicating himself and Dennis*] to help her through that period. So when he starts to have his little fits I just tell him to get out of the house. I don't need it and your mother *certainly* does not need it. Just go outside, run around the park and act like an animal. I don't care, just get out.

PG: So you find yourself with somewhat less patience.

FATHER: Of course, anybody would—when you're trying to take care of a mate who is not feeling well and you've got a 10-year-old average intelligence boy acting like a barbarian around the house.

This is a dicey moment. On the one hand I do not want to say anything that might hurt Dennis or his parents and in general I see their positive attitudes about his abilities as a great resource. On the other hand, for his father to insist that he is of average intelligence amounts to parentifying him, denying his obvious limitations because it would be upsetting to face into them.

PG: Well let's look at that from several angles. When you said, "a 10-year-old average intelligence boy"—intelligence of course is a very big term; it covers a lot of areas, but in terms of language skills he's not average. [*I pause for a response or reaction but parents remain silent.*] I don't mean this to be critical.

MOTHER AND FATHER: Okay, yeah.

PG: We all recognize he is not average.

FATHER: [*Abruptly*] Okay, fine.

PG: He has more difficulty with language than many other children.

FATHER: Why does it always have to come out as whining and a temper tantrum though?

PG: You're asking my opinion?

FATHER: Yeah.

PG: I think there are two reasons. One is that he doesn't have the skills that other people do, other children the same age. And I think from time to time he is frightened. And you put those together and he ends up acting, frankly, like a much younger child.

FATHER: But at times we *do* see the skills; when he's in a real good mood.

PG: I think, if you want my opinion, that Dennis *is* upset in a way that he can't label, about his mom not feeling well. That's my opinion.

[*A long pause*]

MOTHER: Unless he shows it in a different way, Bill.

FATHER: [*Quietly*] I understood that. [*Another pause*] So what do we do about it?

PG: [*To Father*] With your wife being sick it's a stress on you, and I think there's a natural inclination to feel like, "Wait a second, she's sick, it's hard, I'm concerned, I'm worried, perhaps. And why the heck can't you *just behave?*"

I want Mr. S to know that I can see his side and acknowledge his stress and worry, as well as the naturalness of his frustration and anger; I also want him to see that he is perhaps being less patient and understanding than usual and that his expectations for Dennis may be unrealistic. As in earlier exchanges I acknowledge his worry and stress so that he may more readily acknowledge that Dennis might be feeling the same way. My acknowledgment is not intended to be an end-product but a catalyst for change in this family's relationships.

PG: And what I'm thinking is maybe his behavior is pretty much the same, but your tolerance of it is different.

Again I hold Mr. S accountable for his actions and the way they affect other people.

FATHER: Tolerance level is lower.
PG: And maybe he's not any worse—
FATHER: Okay. Yeah.
PG: —but it gets to you more.
FATHER: [*Nodding*] Quicker.

His own difficulties having been acknowledged, it is possible for Mr. S to acknowledge that it is an error to blame Dennis for his short fuse at a time of high stress.

The final section of this therapy session focuses on discussion of a point system that Dennis's parents will try out as a means of increasing his compliance with their requests. The point system is of the standard variety and includes provisions for the accrual of points for good behavior, the loss of points for noncompliance, and a menu of rewards that Dennis may "purchase" with his points. This is one of the many ways that techniques developed within other frameworks, in this case one associated with behavioral approaches, may be usefully incorporated into the contextual approach.

SESSION 10: ONE WEEK LATER

The seeds planted in previous sessions, especially session 9, regarding the need to recognize and make accommodations to Dennis's cognitive limitations, become a focus this week. This leads Dennis's parents, especially his mother, to confront the sense of loss and grieving over their son's cognitive limitations. This session begins with a discussion of a school psychologist's report of a prior year's evaluation of Dennis's intellectual capabilities and limitations. His mother talks about how he has made progress over the past several years. She emphasizes his strengths, including his particularly high marks in spelling and his consistently good behavior. She also talks about a niece who was placed in accelerated classes and experienced discomfort at being "too smart." Dennis's father comments, "He just sees things in a different way. It's not wrong. He gets to the same point that you do; he just gets there in his own way." I do not wish to undermine their pride in his accomplishments but feel that a more realistic appraisal of his capabilities and limitations may alleviate some of the blaming he has experienced.

PG: These school reports seem to suggest that some things are just *extremely* difficult for Dennis, and there may be things that he *simply doesn't* understand, even if he's in a good mood.
MOTHER: Yeah.
PG: And I sense that there must be some feeling of sadness and perhaps loss for his sake.
MOTHER: Yeah. I see my two nieces. They are very smart. They're both in gifted programs and all. And that's nice. It's nice to have kids fall into that category. It makes parents feel

really proud of their kids. All right, my boy is slow. [*Dennis,
who is sitting next to Mother, turns away from her, and is
facing the wall, semi-curled up in his chair. The impression is
one of shame.*] My boy is behind a year or so. [*Mother
reaches out to place her hand on Dennis's shoulder. Dennis
does not move.*] But I feel this way: My Dennis, if you show
him something — [*Dennis turns from the wall toward his
mother*] Dennis is the type of kid, if you show him something
and put it in front of him, or you do it and you say, "Dennis
you've got to do it this way." Dennis will watch you and then
he'll do it. My four nieces, if you want to show them something like that you've got to stand there and show them four
times — and they're smart. [*As his mother talks about his
strengths in being able to do some things well, Dennis uncurls
and turns around so that he is once again facing PG and his
parents. As she returns to the subject of her distress about his
limitations he once again curls up and faces the wall.*] Yes,
some children are very smart. I can tell by the way they talk,
the way they do their work. And yeah that bothers me, because I see my boy, and then I see other kids. But then I think,
I shouldn't let it really bother me. At least he's trying. He's
doing his best, you know. He's doing more now, and getting
more and more awards. [*As Mrs. S continues to talk about
his good work in spelling and other subjects Dennis again
turns away from the wall, this time moving his chair closer to
his mother, uncurling and laying his head on her arm like a
flower unfolding.*]

As the session continues Dennis's mother talks about some of
the difficulties he has experienced in school, including being
teased and bullied by other children on occasion.

PG: Dennis experiences a lot of frustration. School is frustrating. Reading is frustrating. I think speaking is frustrating.
Even here, when I ask Dennis a question, it seems like he sees
me as a friend and that he would like to help me out and

respond in a way that I'm asking for but sometimes he can't because he doesn't understand what I'm asking.

I continue in this vein, taking Dennis's side by pointing out the deficits I have observed. In some instances talking about a child's difficulties at length would be equivalent to scapegoating him; here it serves to inoculate against future scapegoating. If his parents can understand Dennis's actual abilities, if they can accept his limitations, they will be less likely to blame him for failing to do things that are outside his capacities; they will also be better able to help him maximize his potential.

MOTHER: Yeah.
PG: I can't help wondering if the temper tantrums—
MOTHER: Is the way he's showing his frustration.
PG: Yeah.

This point, that Dennis's tantrums may result from his frustration in communication, is of course where the therapy started several months earlier. When I first brought up this possibility, during the crisis-provoked family evaluation session, Mr. and Mrs. S tentatively and somewhat reluctantly agreed that it might be possible. At this point it appears that they have integrated this idea into their understanding of their son. Later in the session Mr. and Mrs. S report that they had planned to begin using the point system we discussed last week, but that things had been going so much better that it had not been necessary. They felt that they could wait two weeks for their next appointment for the same reason.

SESSION 11: TWO WEEKS LATER

As this session begins, Dennis's parents explain that they have grounded Dennis because he went to a carnival along with some other boys from his apartment complex. This adventure involved crossing a major highway on a pedestrian catwalk, something that they had explicitly forbidden. This rule violation provides an opportunity to continue the previous session's discussion of the ways that Dennis's cognitive limitations affect daily life and how some things that may appear to be defiance or other intentionally bad behavior may instead reflect these limitations.

PG: When the other boys asked you to go—[*Dennis looks a bit blank*] the other boys, when they said, "We're going to the carnival," did you remember that your mother and father had said not to go?

DENNIS: [*Putting his hands up to his face*] I forgot.

PG: You forgot. [*To parents*] The reason I asked, and of course it's a very hard thing for us to know whether that's just a convenient thing to say or whether it's true, is that I did get some materials from school from the evaluation they just completed. I understand that they went over them with you?

MOTHER AND FATHER: Mmm hmm.

PG: The reports say that memory is a difficult area for Dennis and I wonder if maybe he really did forget.

FATHER: We worry about him when he's out and we're trying to get him to see that the rules are there to make sure he's safe.

PG: Dennis, do you understand now that your parents were worried about you?

DENNIS: Yes.

PG: And do you know why they were worried?

DENNIS: [*Initially smiles, then looks from one adult to another but remains silent. It becomes apparent that he is confused.*]

PG: I didn't ask the question correctly.

I decide to be explicit about my responsibility for this in order to head off blaming of Dennis for not paying attention.

FATHER: He didn't understand the question.

Mr. S's comment is remarkable for its sympathetic tone. He does not blame Dennis for failing to pay attention, but registers his son's comprehension problem.

PG: Yeah. Do you think he understood what I asked about being worried?

FATHER: About us being worried?

PG: Yeah.

FATHER: No.

[*Dennis, like his father, is sitting with his arms crossed over his chest.*]

PG: Okay. [*To Dennis*] Your mother and father were afraid that you might get hurt. Did you know that?

DENNIS: [*After a silence of some seconds, tentatively*] Yeah.

PG: Do you know what I mean?

DENNIS: [*Shakes his head and smiles.*]

PG: Maybe Dad can help me. [*Dennis turns and looks expectantly and attentively at his father.*] How would that be, if Dad helped me with what I'm trying to say?

I am genuinely having a bit of difficulty communicating with Dennis at this point; my major motivation, however, is to give room to Mr. S to help Dennis, room for him to earn constructive entitlement by actively considering and responding to his son's needs. Were I to have persevered and ultimately succeeded in making my point to Dennis, Mr. S's opportunity would have been lost.

FATHER: [*Uncrossing his arms and leaning toward Dennis*] The night that you went over to the carnival, you were supposed to be someplace else. Right?

DENNIS: Yeah.

FATHER: Where were you supposed to be?

DENNIS: Home.

FATHER: No. When you went to your friend's house, you were supposed to be up there. We came up to your friend's house looking for you; you weren't there. Your friend's mother had seen you going over toward the carnival. We were worried about you crossing the highway and being over there by yourself. Okay?

DENNIS: Mmm hmm.

FATHER: Did you think about it? Did you think we would be worried that you would be out that late?

DENNIS: I don't understand.

This is the first time Dennis has said that he does not understand, his usual response being, "I don't know." I believe that Dennis has begun to respond to the increased support, compassion, and understanding his parents, and especially his father, have shown to him regarding his disability; these changes appear to have enabled Dennis to be more forthright when he is genuinely perplexed.

PG: In this school material, as I read it, what they are saying is that Dennis has some significant problems in perceiving, understanding, and in thinking about certain kinds of things, and that affects his schoolwork. They also say that he's a hard worker, so he does pretty well anyway.

MOTHER: Yes, he does.

PG: But I wondered if that was your perception too. That there are some things that really are difficult for him.

MOTHER: They told us that we would have to repeat to him, what is it, twice?

FATHER: At least twice, sometimes more.

PG: [*To Mother*] You have done so much for Dennis, and it's so important to you to be the kind of mother not just that you want to be, but also that maybe that you wish you had had yourself.

MOTHER: Yeah.

PG: And yet in spite of everything you do for him you see that he has some difficulties.

MOTHER: Oh yeah.

PG: And I would think that would be sad for you.

MOTHER: Yeah. I understand that Dennis is dyslexic. I have two nephews like that. One just graduated last week; he is 19. Dennis will be the same age when he graduates. My other nephew will also be 19 when he graduates. [*Mr. S sits in silence, elbows on knees, looking at the floor. Dennis looks intently at his mother.*] It's not that they're stupid or anything, it's that they can't comprehend. But if you show them, then they comprehend. They're not dumb. They're bright. They are smart in their own ways. They can do things. But grade-wise Dennis has picked up a lot in the last year. Yes, he works hard, very hard, which I'm proud of, especially in spelling. He's excellent in spelling.

DENNIS: I'm good at social studies.

PG: You're good at social studies too?

DENNIS: [*Mumbles something about being good; the specific content is intelligible.*]

FATHER: [*Sits up, looks at Dennis.*]

PG: Dennis, could you say that again?

Anything Dennis says about his own strengths and achievements is too precious to pass over; I ask him to repeat it to ensure that it will not be lost.

DENNIS: I'm good at science and social studies.

PG: [*Joining in*] Both science and social studies.

I repeat Dennis's statement for the same reason, to emphasize and underscore his achievements and by extension to give credit to his parents for helping him in those achievements.

MOTHER: Plus they also told us that if Dennis keeps his grades up that when he's in ninth grade he can go to one of the voc-tec schools. I mean, here they are telling *us* already all these years ahead, because he tries so hard and his grades are good for his level, plus he is very well-behaved in school. They have never had any problems and I've never had to come to school about him because of any kind of problem. And it makes me feel really good that they said he could go to one of these schools. So Dennis asked me about the schools, he asked me, "What kind of schools are they, Mom?" and I said, "It's a school where you can learn a trade." I said, "Dennis you are lucky to be offered this. I was never offered that; even though my grades were Bs and Cs. I was never offered that.

PG: [*Speaking to Father*] I would like to ask your thoughts about this, about school, Dennis's abilities, and his effort.

FATHER: No complaints. The only thing I mentioned to the teachers when we had our meeting is that he has to be motivated constantly because his attention span is so short. That showed up on the report card. I mean one A, one B, and the rest Cs. You can't ask for anything better than that. The only thing I've told him from day one is, "Just go in and do your best." That's all anyone can ask of anyone else; just to do your best. He's coming home with an A. His first A ever.

MOTHER: And he likes spelling and reading. Even though he'll grumble about reading, he likes it. And social studies and science.

DENNIS: I hate handwriting.

MOTHER: You'll learn handwriting more as you go along.

DENNIS: [*Moving his right hand as if writing*] I can't hold the pencil.

PG: It's hard to hold the pencil?

DENNIS: We have the pencil. We doing the work, we have to do it, right. She saying, you finish she give you a clean sheet. That you can rest your arm.

PG: You're tired.

DENNIS: Yeah. I draw with this hand and I messed up. [*Holding up his left arm.*]

PG: Which hand do you usually write with?

DENNIS: My right.

PG: But you got tired and so you wrote with your left hand?

DENNIS: [*With a little laugh*] I tried.

PG: It's hard isn't it?

DENNIS: [*Nods.*]

PG: It sounds like Dennis really does want to do well.

MOTHER: Oh yeah.

PG: And I think he also wants to do well at home.

MOTHER: Mmm hmm.

SESSION 12: TWO WEEKS LATER

The session begins with a recapitulation of the previous session's discussion of the rules regarding crossing the highway without adult supervision and more generally of the issue of helping Dennis remember rules.

PG: Have you come up with some ideas to help Dennis remember the rules so that if somebody says, "Let's go here, let's go there," he will remember and not get in trouble?

MOTHER: Hey Dennis, put your hands down. [*Dennis is holding his hands over his eyes, making the owl face; he seems to be trying to hide his face during the discussion of his "rule violation."*] What did we talk to you about the other day?

DENNIS: [*Looking confused, shakes his head as if to clear his thoughts.*]

MOTHER: Remember, I said when you go out . . . [*long pause*]

DENNIS: Tell, tell where you at.

PG: Tell who?

DENNIS: Tell Mom where you go, or Dad.

MOTHER: And what else?

DENNIS: After you ask first, go somewhere.

MOTHER: Yeah. And what else did we say? If something goes wrong . . . [*pause*]

DENNIS: Tell the truth.

MOTHER: And what else? Not to go where? Why did you stay in for those 19 days?

DENNIS: Carnival.

MOTHER: So you're not allowed to do what?

DENNIS: To the carnival.

FATHER: [*Very gently*] Well, the carnival is not there now.

MOTHER: The carnival is not there but you're not allowed to go where? How did you get over there?

DENNIS: Walk on the catwalk.

MOTHER: You're not allowed to go where? Across the highway, right?

DENNIS: Yeah.

MOTHER: He's been doing better. He came in on time last night. I told him when he had to be back in, and he was in.

PG: So do you feel that things are going better with Dennis in terms of following rules?

MOTHER: When he follows the rules, yeah. But at times there are some things that throw him off.

PG: When he remembers the rules he does okay.

MOTHER: Yeah.

FATHER: But a lot of times it's reinforcing the rules over and over and over and over.

PG: I think so. Probably just as the school said, "over and over and over."

FATHER: You keep on going and after a while the rules sink in. That starts to get on our nerves too.

PG: You mean to have to keep repeating it?

FATHER: Over and over and over.

PG: It's hard to be that patient.

I acknowledge the effort and patience required to convey new information to Dennis.

FATHER: Uh huh, but that's what it requires to be a parent. You've got to *be* that patient. You've got to *force* yourself to be that patient, which no human being is automatically. You just have to *force* yourself to be that patient.

PG: It is hard work. Does it feel like it's worth it?

FATHER: Yeah. You can see this difference in him. I can see the difference in him.

PG: So you're really happier with him if you put in the effort, happier with how the whole family is going.

MOTHER: Yeah.

FATHER: Oh, yeah. Sure. If I didn't want to put in the effort, I wouldn't be here.

The previous exchange between Mr. S and myself encapsulates the essence of the contextual approach. Mr. S accurately labels the effort required to be a patient parent. In saying that he wants to put in the effort, that he sees that as part of being a parent, Mr. S highlights his own reliance on constructive entitlement; by giving more to Dennis, by helping Dennis more, his own sense of self-worth and self-valuation has increased.

[Later in the session]

PG: You had mentioned Grandmother earlier and one of the things we had touched on was whether there was anything that you would like to see change about things with your mother. Several months ago you had said you really didn't want to get into that. So I would just like to ask if your thoughts about that have changed.

MOTHER: No, not really.

PG: I keep thinking that perhaps if there were some possibility of things being even a tiny bit better—I'm not expecting, to tell you the truth, any big changes to be possible—your mother is who she is.

MOTHER: Yeah.

PG: But if it were possible for things to be maybe a tiny bit better, would that be of some benefit to Dennis, to have in some way two grandmothers; your mother [*gesturing to Father*], and your mother [*gesturing to Mother*]? Even if growing up he may look back and say, "One grandmother was this, and the other was, well, difficult."

I suggest that there may be some benefits to Dennis if Mrs. S can resolve some of the long-standing difficulties between herself and her mother. By the time we have reached this session there are numerous indications that therapy is winding down. Mr. and Mrs. S have few complaints about Dennis's behavior or lack of responsibility; to the contrary, they have many more positive than negative comments about him. They have begun to request sessions every other week instead of every week and have canceled several of those. I believe that I may have few, if any, additional opportunities to encourage some positive movement in Mrs. S's very conflictual and painful relationship with her mother. For this reason I choose to make these remarks despite Mrs S's saying that she has no great interest in working on that relationship.

The next session, scheduled for two weeks later, was missed but Mr. S reported by telephone that things were going very well, and that Dennis had been "doing chores he never would have done in a million years." The session was rescheduled for the following week. Mrs. S called to cancel this session, saying that things were going very well and that they did not feel a need to meet but that they would call in the future at any time when they felt it would be helpful.

9

FOLLOW-UP SESSIONS WITH THE S FAMILY

Approximately four months after the final family session Mrs. S called to ask for an appointment to talk about her relationship with her mother.

SESSION 13: FOUR MONTHS LATER

Before beginning to talk about her and her mother Mrs. S brings me up to date on Dennis.

MOTHER: Dennis is a little stubborn at times but he is doing well. We're giving him a little bit more responsibility. There will be times that I'm not home and he comes home from school by himself. Sometimes my husband is there. Last Monday he was getting out of school early, so I gave him door-keys. He came in. He was fine, you know. We're beginning to trust him more, that he can be by himself and do things. He went out on Halloween with a bunch of other people but he went all over the area. He's getting bigger and I know it. We're letting him go as long as he tells us the truth and there are no problems, then things will be all right. He's doing well in school except one teacher gave him a bad grade and I had to go back and tell her. She said, "Well I didn't know about this problem with Dennis." I said, "I told you the second week in September. See, Dennis is diagnosed now with cerebral palsy. When I was told back in August, that crushed me. I mean for a week I cried, but I never thought and I never saw anything. No one really noticed it. I took him to his family doctor and other doctors and they never [*shakes her head*]. And he [*family doctor*] said, "Yeah, I could tell." All Dennis feels is that he is slow and that it takes him a while to catch on to things. My husband never thought any different. He felt bad, but then he felt, well that's Dennis. Then, when was it, in September I saw my Uncle, late in September I think it was, Yeah. Dennis and I did. And then my mother called me and I told her about it. I've been talking to my mom for about a month now. It isn't there any more; no feelings. I can't understand why I don't have any feelings for her. I don't even hardly want to be around her. She's gotten sick and things have gone wrong with her. Two and a half weeks ago she was in the hospital and she had a few things done, but it seems like what she wants is for everybody to do things for her; she wants to depend on everybody else. I came out and told her, "Well you can't do that. You've got to learn to do on your own and do like you used to, Mom." She said, "I can't anymore." I said, "Well you have to." I don't know, I can't understand why. [*Pause*] I love her. In a way I do and in a way I don't. I don't really care about being around her. Every time I get off the phone after talking to her or seeing her, I get so upset that I could destroy something. Last night we had an argument on the phone. I said, "Listen you let yourself get depressed, get sick, you won't get up and do anything."

PG: When you told your mother about Dennis having cerebral palsy did you hope that she would understand how that would hurt you, that she might say or do something to show you she cared?

MOTHER: Yeah I did, but she didn't. She only talked about herself, how she couldn't do this, how she needed help.

PG: That would really hurt.

MOTHER: Yeah, it hurt a lot.

Mrs. S continues to hope that her mother will change in ways that will help their relationship to improve. She appears to be deeply disappointed and hurt when she finds that her mother is incapable of responding in a caring or considerate way to her distress over learning that her son has cerebral palsy. And yet even the pain of this disappointment is not enough to push Mrs. S into cutting off all hope of a better relationship with her mother.

SESSION 14: ONE WEEK LATER

MOTHER: Dennis has to go to court in two weeks.

PG: He does?

MOTHER: He didn't do anything. He was a witness.

PG: What happened?

MOTHER: He was with a couple of boys, around three months ago, and they were throwing rocks, and one of the rocks hit a car. I asked if Dennis had thrown the rocks. They said, "No, he just stood there. He froze." I'm going to have to explain to the people in court that they're going to have to put their questions at a little easier level for Dennis because of his cerebral palsy. I don't know if I should let the court know that ahead of time or what. If that affects the testimony or what, because you really have to explain to Dennis for him to comprehend. But I said, "Dennis, all you have to do is explain what happened, that's it."

[*Later in the session*]

MOTHER: I haven't talked to my mom. I just haven't bothered. I feel happier when I'm away from her. When I'm around her, it just isn't there. I don't know if it's all because of the past. I don't know but I think it is. It's always got to be her way, if it isn't her way she would lash out. Three months ago—no, it was the middle of May—Dennis came home from school and he said, "There was this lady who came to school to ask me questions." It was a lady from the child protection agency, and he said why? And so I told him that apparently he had gotten a bruise on his leg and somebody saw it. She went to school to talk to Dennis before she came here to talk to me. When she came to talk to me she said she asked him how he got the bruises. Dennis told me that she asked him how he got the bruises and he told her it was from running and playing. And then she asked, "Are you sure that somebody didn't hit you?" And he said "No." When the lady came here she asked about Dennis's and his father's feelings for each other. And so I told her that they have their arguments but that they love each other. Dennis is very close to him. After we talked, about two weeks later, they closed the case. And Dennis said to me, "Mom, she was asking me if you hit me, if Daddy hits me, do you always yell at me all the time?" I asked what he told her, and he said, "I told her no." He told me that he told her, "I love my mom and dad. They do things for me. They do more things for me than my mom's mom did for her when she was growing up." She asked him, "What do you mean by that?" He said, "My grandmother was mean toward my mother, even when she got older." And she said, "Dennis, how do you know that?" And he said, "I remember even when I was younger, I remember my grandmother would always yell at my mom; she would beat my mom three times and I know." And he said, "I love my grandmother but I don't want to see her, because she hurt my mom." She *has* hurt me a lot, but I have learned to go on, and I have my husband and I have my son. They help fill the emptiness. And I have my mother-in-law.

PG: It sounds like you still want to help her.

While Mrs. S describes how she has been hurt by her mother her tone and other nonverbal channels of communication convey regret, sadness, disappointment, and anger; there is still a strong undercurrent of caring and wishing for something better. It is this caring and hope for the future that I hope to enhance by my comment.

MOTHER: Yes, I do. I tried for days and weeks and then we had a big argument on the phone and I just got disgusted. She puts on a front. I can read her like a book. Out of all the kids I understand her more than anybody. But I can't trust her anymore like I used to. Everything was fine for a while. And then in January when I told her, "Dennis has to have help." And she said, "No." I said, "Look, I'm not going to have my son standing up to me when he's 15 and walk all over me and bring the cops to my door or anything like that." And she told me I was a child abuser and that I neglected Dennis and I never took care of him. And that's when the whole ball of wax just exploded.

PG: These kind of statements also bring up the whole question of your mother's illness. I'm not making excuses for her, but it seems like that's an important thing.

I take Mrs. S's descriptions of her mother's behavior very seriously; in other words, I hold her accountable for what she says.

MOTHER: Oh yeah. She does have a problem. But she won't admit to it. When you don't admit to it you aren't doing yourself any good. When she goes, I don't know if I'll be able to be there for her the way I was for my dad. My dad never said the things to me that she has. My dad gave me credit for what I did for him and for Dennis.

Mrs. S's statements provide a wonderfully lucid example of how being exploited and hurt can result in impediments to one's capacity to give to another. She worries that her mother has hurt her so badly and so often that she may find herself incapable of being the loving and considerate daughter she wants to be. When her father was dying Mrs. S was able to care for him, something that made her feel good about herself as a daughter. Now, as her mother has increasing medical problems, Mrs. S worries that she may find herself incapable of giving to her as she did to her father; she worries that all the resentment and anger that has resulted from being so badly hurt so many times may block her ability to give to her mother.

[*Later in the session after she has talked about various ways in which her mother has hurt her in the past.*]

MOTHER: That hurt me a lot. My dad took it very hard when his mother died. I think he went to his grave grieving for her. I never knew his father. My dad saw tragedy all his life too. And he learned to go on, but when his mother died, that hurt him. And when my mom gave up on their marriage, that really hurt him. Because he didn't have his mother or his father around any more, and all of us kids were out and on our own. Which was not easy to do, because my mother tried to keep us all at home; she didn't want us to have any kind of a life of our own.

This statement illuminates our understanding of Mrs. S's bind regarding her conflict with her mother. In addition to the physical and emotional pain she has endured, Mrs. S has been placed in a split loyalty bind following her parents' divorce. She feels great sympathy for her father for the losses in his life; she blames her mother for hurting him by "giving up on their marriage."

SESSION 15: THREE YEARS LATER

Mrs. S.'s mother died approximately three years after the previous session. Several months after her death, and coincidental with the writing of this chapter, Mrs. S called to request an appointment, saying that Dennis had asked to talk to me about his grandmother and his grief over her death. She also explained that there had been an incident on the school bus in which another boy had said something insulting about her, and Dennis, leaping to her defense, had pushed the other youngster and had been suspended from school for three days as punishment. Apparently many of Mrs. S's relatives and friends had the point of view that he had really done the decent thing in defending his mother. Mrs. S agreed with this but emphasized that the appropriate way for him to respond to such offenses was "with words," not by pushing.

During this session Dennis talked about how much he missed his grandmother. Mrs. S mentioned her previous difficulties with her mother but stressed that she felt good because she had been able to help her mother during her illness and because Dennis had been able to have some closeness with his grandmother. In addition, Mrs. S expressed concerns that Dennis had begun to be a bit "mouthy" at home, especially with his father. In talking with Dennis it appeared that he had experienced growing frustration in school over the past year. This impression was borne out by Dennis's complaints that his teachers do not give him enough time to respond to questions and to complete in-class assignments and that the work is "too hard." His mother explained that she had been told that Dennis's spelling abilities are so strong that they considered him to be a "borderline savant." We explored the possibility that this frustration in school might be responsible for Dennis's anger and oppositional behavior at home. At the end of the session Dennis and his mother requested an additional appointment for the following week; his father will also attend if his work schedule permits.

EPILOGUE

The overview of therapy with the S family puts an interesting perspective on the question of treatment length. So far I have met with the S family 15 times over a three-year period. Is this long-term therapy because it has been three years since the initial session? Or is it short-term therapy because there have been only 15 sessions? And by extension, since I am offering this case study as an illustration of contextual therapy, does this mean that contextual therapy is short-term, medium-term, or long-term therapy?

I hope that this case, together with the other cases in this book, demonstrates that contextual therapy is not preoccupied with treatment length. It is neither short- nor long-term. Perhaps the best way to define it would be as long-enough-term. Mr. and Mrs. S may continue to check in with me over the years, but if they do so it will be in the same way that they may return to their family doctor, not as people whose therapy was unsuccessful and so needs repeating, but as a family who may benefit from some help with intermittent difficulties. In fact, the image of a family doctor may not be a bad one for the sort of therapy that is described here. My role was much more like that of a pediatrician or family doctor who a family consults as the need arises, rather than that of a specialist who is called in to resolve an acute problem but never seen again.

10

THE ESSENCE OF
CONTEXTUAL THERAPY

Looking back, it feels that I have spent almost as many words writing about what contextual therapy is *not* as in defining what it *is*. I have said that it is not an individual therapy and yet have argued that one should not think of it just as a form of family therapy either. We have seen that contrary to popular opinion contextual therapy is not properly thought of as being a long-term approach, and yet it is not properly short-term either, at least not as defined by currently more visible short-term approaches.

We contextual therapists appear to have wrapped ourselves in a cloak of contradictions. We eschew focusing on pathology but emphasize the need for accurate diagnosis and the importance of having a detailed history. We are concerned about relationships but are willing to accept someone's preference that he work with us alone on marital difficulties. We are concerned about the parentification and scapegoating of children but may allow this to continue in our presence for some time in certain cases.

The apparent contradictions continue. We emphasize the integration of psychodynamic concepts and techniques into our work and yet we rarely, if ever, comment on or interpret the transferential aspects of patients' remarks or behavior. We do not routinely ask patients to report their dreams, and yet readers may be wondering if this is also permissible under the contextual canopy. (In fact it is.)

So, ultimately, what are we left with? What is the essence of contextual therapy? We have seen several examples of change — sometimes, as in the case of Dennis and his family, fairly dramatic change in a short period of time. But how does change come about?

The answer to this question provides a useful framework for reviewing our journey. Of the four dimensions that comprise the contextual framework, we clearly rely largely on the fourth, the one I have sometimes referred to as the dimension of fairness in relationships, sometimes as the dimension of the ethics of close relationships. We rely on the other three dimensions (history, psychology, and transactions) to contribute to, bolster, implement, and develop our understanding of the balance or imbalance in these close relationships.

Contextual therapy rests on two pillars: A commitment to identifying and building on interpersonal resources and strengths and an equally fundamental commitment to helping people find and utilize opportunities to contribute to others, most especially those in their families. These principles underlie and subsume all other goals and techniques. We work hard to identify and acknowledge each person's efforts to be helpful as a way of helping our patients to do the same, and as a way of initiating a benign cycle of acknowledgment, enhanced self-worth, and increased freedom to give to others. We look for openings to help people increase their sensitivities to each other and to act in ways that consider other people's difficult experiences and current needs, feelings, and aspirations.

We learn how someone has suffered pain or loss in the past and begin to understand their difficulty in empathically responding to another's difficulties now. Or we learn about a child's cognitive limitations, and understand his mother's guilt and his own frustration, anger, and the resulting disruptive behavior as all reflecting the unfairness of the situation. Having learned about this hurt in the past, we are able to more accurately and effectively take the person's side. In some instances this means expressing our own empathic response to their suffering. In others it means helping a tentative, self-deprecating man to be more assertive with his wife. In some it means helping a person to see how what he says and does affects other people. And in still others it means helping a learning disabled, autistic, or developmentally delayed youngster express himself in a family session.

We observe how two people enter the office, where and how they sit, how they speak and listen (or do not listen) to each other and learn about the quality of the relationship and how well they communicate with each other. If we comment on these transactional patterns, we do so to help the people understand each other so that they can have a dialogue and arrive at solutions to their problems and compromises in the face of their conflicts. If we place ourselves transactionally between them, we do so to serve as a temporary translator, also to facilitate a dialogue between them. And if we make specific suggestions regarding possible changes in the way they talk to each other, we do so to help both people to state their own sides clearly so that they may work together to achieve a more balanced relationship.

If we hear parents denigrating or blaming young children, if we see them smirking while a young child struggles to express herself, we interrupt the scapegoating process and emphasize the importance of the child's contributions to the family and to the family session. Scapegoating is a form of blaming and parentification and if continued will gradually block the child's capacity to give as surely as silt blocks the mouth of a river. We interrupt the scapegoating to keep the child's opportunities to give to her family, and so her opportunities to build her own self-esteem, open.

Some, perhaps many, may be wondering how one learns to do this. This book has tried to provide more than the bare bones of the approach, and to describe at least some techniques in sufficient detail that a seasoned clinician will feel comfortable trying them out. But mastering a new therapeutic model requires more than a book, no matter how clinical and practical it sets out to be. Seminars and workshops of the sort typically presented in conjunction with professional conferences can be quite helpful in providing opportunities for discussions with practitioners of the approach and may also include the opportunity to view videotaped or in vivo therapy sessions. Videotapes of sessions conducted by senior contextual therapists may be rented or purchased for repeated study. Institutes and centers throughout the United States and Europe offer courses, workshops, and seminars that can be very helpful in developing facility with the approach. But ultimately anyone who sees sufficient value in this approach to strive toward mastery would be well advised to look for a setting in which he or she can receive regular supervision on his or her own cases. In addition, regardless of whether personal therapy is required by one's training program or supervisor, there can be little doubt about the value to a contextual therapist of sorting out one's own personal and family issues.

REFERENCES

Ackerman, N. W. (1966). *Treating the troubled family*. New York: Basic.

Adler, A. (1923). *Superiority and social interest*. New York: Norton.

Adler, A. (1924). *The practice and theory of individual psychology*. New York: Putnam.

Adler, A. (1927). *Understanding human nature*. New York: Fawcett.

Ayto, J. (1990). *Dictionary of Word Origins*. New York: Arcade.

Bateson, G. (1972). *Steps to an ecology of mind*. New York: Chandler.

Bateson, G., Jackson, D. D., Haley, J., & Weakland, J. H. (1956). Toward a theory of schizophrenia. *Behavioral Science, 1*, 251–254.

Beck, A. T., Rush, A. J., Shaw, A. J., & Emery, G. (1979). *Cognitive therapy of depression*. New York: Guilford.

Bernal, G., Rodríguez, C., & Diamond, G. (1990). Contextual therapy: Brief treatment of an addict and spouse. *Family Process, 29*, 59–71.

Boszormenyi-Nagy, I. (1965). A theory of relationships: Experience and transaction. In I. Boszormenyi-Nagy & J. L. Framo (Eds.), *Intensive family therapy*. New York: Brunner/Mazel.

Boszormenyi-Nagy, I. (1987). *Foundations of contextual therapy: Collected Papers of Ivan Boszormenyi-Nagy, M.D.* New York: Brunner/Mazel.

Boszormenyi-Nagy, I., & Krasner, B. (1986). *Between give and take: A clinical guide to contextual therapy*. New York: Brunner/Mazel.

Boszormenyi-Nagy, I., Grunebaum, J., & Ulrich, D. (1991). Contextual therapy. In A. Gurman & D. P. Kniskern (Eds.), *Handbook of family therapy. Volume II.* New York: Brunner/Mazel.

Boszormenyi-Nagy, I., & Spark, G. M. (1973). *Invisible loyalties.* New York: Harper & Row.

Bowen, M. (1966). The use of family therapy in clinical practice. *Comprehensive Psychiatry, 7*, 345–374.

Bowen, M. (1978). *Family therapy in clinical practice.* New York: Jason Aronson.

Burbatti, G. L., Castoldi, I., & Maggi, L. (1993). *Systemic psychotherapy with families, couples, and individuals.* Northvale, NJ: Jason Aronson.

de Shazer, S. (1991). *Putting difference to work.* New York: Norton.

Erikson, E. H. (1963). *Childhood and society.* New York: Norton.

Erikson, E. H. (1968). *Identity: Youth and crisis.* New York: Norton

Flavell, J. H. (1977). *Cognitive development.* New York: Prentice-Hall.

Framo, J. L. (1976). Family of origin as a resource for adults in marital and family therapy: You can and should go home again. *Family Process, 15*, 193–210.

Framo, J. L. (1982). *Explorations in family and marital therapy.* New York: Springer.

Freud, A. (1946). *The ego and the mechanisms of defense.* New York: International Universities Press.

Frith, U. (Ed.). (1991). *Autism and Asperger syndrome.* Cambridge: Cambridge University Press.

Furman, B., & Tapani, A. (1992). *Solution talk: Hosting therapeutic conversations.* New York: Norton.

Garfield, S. (1994). Eclecticism and integration in psychotherapy: Developments and issues. *Clinical Psychology: Science and Practice, 1*, 123–137.

Goldenthal, P. (1993). *Contextual family therapy: Assessment and intervention procedures.* Sarasota: Professional Resource Press.

Goldfried, M. R. (1980). Toward the delineation of therapeutic change principles. *American Psychologist, 35*, 991–999.

Goldfried, M. R. (Ed.). (1982). *Converging themes in psychotherapy.* New York: Springer.

Greenberg, J. R., & Mitchell, S. A. (1983). *Object relations in psychoanalytic theory.* Cambridge, MA: Harvard University Press.

Gurman, A. S., & Kniskern, D. P. (Eds.). (1981). *Handbook of family therapy.* New York: Brunner/Mazel.

Gurman, A. S., & Kniskern, D. P. (Eds.). (1991). *Handbook of family therapy. Volume II.* New York: Brunner/Mazel.

Haley, J. (1976). *Problem solving therapy.* San Fransisco: Jossey-Bass.

Hynd, G. E., & Willis, W. G. (1988). *Pediatric neuropsychology.* New York: Grune & Stratton.

Jackson, D. D. (1957). The question of family homeostasis. *Psychiatric Quarterly, 31*, 79–90.

Kaplan, H. S. (1974). *The new sex therapy: Active treatment of sexual dysfunctions.* New York: Brunner/Mazel.

Kazdin, A. E. (1995). Scope of child and adolescent psychotherapy research: Limited sampling of dysfunctions, treatments, and client characteristics. *Journal of Child Clinical Psychology, 24*, 125–140.

Kerr, M. E., & Bowen, M. (1988). *Family evaluation: An approach based on Bowen theory.* New York: Norton.

Levant, R. F. (1984). *Family therapy: A comprehensive overview.* Englewood Cliffs, NJ: Prentice-Hall.

Levine, M. D. (1991). The subspeciality of developmental-behavioral pediatrics. Presidential address. *Journal of Developmental & Behavioral Pediatrics, 12,* 1–3.

Minuchin, S. (1974). *Families and family therapy.* Cambridge, MA: Harvard University Press.

Norcross, J., & Goldfried, M. (1992). *Handbook of psychotherapy integration.* New York: Basic.

Piaget, J. (1963). *The origins of intelligence.* New York: Norton.

Piaget, J., & Inhelder, B. (1969). *The psychology of the child.* New York: Basic.

Rotter, J. B. (1954). *Social learning and clinical psychology.* New York: Prentice-Hall.

Sacks, O. (1995). *An anthropologist on Mars: Seven paradoxical tales.* New York: Knopf.

Selvini-Palazzoli, M., Boscolo, L., Cecchin, G., & Prata, G. (1978). *Paradox and counterparadox: A new model in the therapy of the family in schizophrenic transaction.* New York: Jason Aronson.

Selvini-Palazzoli, M., Boscolo, L., Cecchin, G., & Prata, G. (1980). Hypothesizing-circularity-neutrality: Three guidelines for the conductor of the session. *Family Process, 19,* 3–12.

Stricker, G. (1994). Reflections of psychotherapy integration. *Clinical Psychology: Science and Practice, 1,* 3–12.

Sullivan, H. S. (1953). *The interpersonal theory of psychiatry.* New York: Norton.

van Heusden, A., & van den Eerenbeemt, E. (1987). *Balance in motion: Ivan Boszormenyi-Nagy and his vision of individual and family therapy.* New York: Brunner/Mazel.

Wynne, L. C. (1965). Some indications and contraindications for exploratory family therapy. In I. Boszormenyi-Nagy & J. L. Framo (Eds.), *Intensive family therapy: Theoretical and practical aspects.* New York: Harper & Row.

Wynne, L. C., Ryckoff, I. M., Day, J., & Hirsch, S. I. (1958). Pseudomutuality in the family relations of schizophrenics. *Psychiatry, 21,* 205–220.

INDEX